The Spirit of Rural
IRELAND

The Spirit of Rural
IRELAND

CHRISTOPHER SOMERVILLE
PHOTOGRAPHY BY CHRIS COE
FOREWORD BY DERVLA MURPHY

NEW HOLLAND

First published in 2001 by New Holland Publishers (UK) Ltd
London ● Cape Town ● Sydney ● Auckland

1 3 5 7 9 10 8 6 4 2

Garfield House, 86-88 Edgware Road, London W2 2EA,
United Kingdom
www.newhollandpublishers.com

80 McKenzie Street, Cape Town 8001, South Africa

14 Aquatic Drive, Frenchs Forest, NSW 2086, Australia

218 Lake Road, Northcote, Auckland, New Zealand

Copyright © 2001 in text: Christopher Somerville

Copyright © 2001 in photographs: Chris Coe
other than page 47 lower right R.T. Mills

Copyright © 2001 New Holland Publishers (UK) Ltd

ISBN 1 85974 882 1 (HB)
ISBN 1 85974 956 9 (PB)

Publishing Manager: Jo Hemmings
Project Editor: Mike Unwin
Designer, Copy Editor & Cover Design: Design Revolution
Production: Joan Woodroffe

Reproduction by Pica Digital Pte Ltd, Singapore

Printed and bound in Singapore by Kyodo Printing Co (Singapore)
Pte Ltd

Cover image: Cottage at Maumturk Cross, Co. Galway

Back cover image: Ceilidh at Fernagh, Co. Tyrone

page 1: Roundstone harbour, Co. Galway

page 2: Farm near Ventry, Dingle, Co. Kerry

page 5: Dunluce Castle, Co. Antrim

page 6: Painted cart and old milk churns near Ennis, Co. Clare

page 7: vignetted image – Olcan Masterson

page 7: l–r: Dancer at Fleadh Nua, Ennis, Co. Clare;

painted shutters, Co. Cork; donkey looking over a wall,

Co. Galway; bric-a-brac shop, Ennis, Co. Clare;

boats in Rossaveal harbour, Co. Galway

page 8: Standing stones, Carrowmore, Co. Sligo

CONTENTS

FOREWORD

by Dervla Murphy

At first glance, I feared that this might be yet another sentimental drool over a quaint misty island populated by fairies, leprechauns and stage Irishmen and women. In fact it is an effective antidote to such volumes, partly because of Christopher Somerville's intimate knowledge of Irish history and culture, partly because of his modus operandi. He observes only as a walker can, noticing those tiny, fragile, momentary beauties inevitably missed by motorists – or even cyclists. And many of the rural folk he meets en route befriend him as they would not befriend motorists, independent and isolated in their metal boxes.

Within the past decade, Ireland has developed a split personality. The country has become rich – among the richest in Europe – and the abruptness of this change, however beneficial it may be in some respects, has had a traumatic effect. Countries, like individuals, find it hard to handle the equivalent of a major lottery prize. So now we have two Irelands, mutually antagonistic on certain levels, most notably when it comes to protecting natural beauty from indiscriminate development. One is known, rather inanely, as 'the Celtic Tiger'. The other might be prosaically described as 'traditional Ireland', the Ireland Christopher Somerville sought and found at the turn of the millennium. Occasionally he indicates this divide, as when a Connemara farmer tells him, '...the government and the EU hand us down some subsidies. That's what keeps us going... All the tourists want is for the landscape to stay as it is, beautiful and wild. But I think most of the people in Connemara would tell you they would rather see some factories built, even if it spoils the scenery.'

Christopher Somerville resolutely ignores or evades the horrors of uncontrolled ribbon-building, the twee suburbanization of small towns and villages, the ravaging of many counties by four-lane highways and golf courses, the proliferation of superfluous signposts and mindless hoardings. Of these last the most mindless remind tourists, in several languages, to drive on the left – and are often to be seen forty or fifty miles from the nearest port, when motorists who had not already absorbed that message would no longer be driving on either side of the road. My own little home-town – Lismore, Co. Waterford – has had the misfortune to be designated a 'Heritage Town' on which EU funds (sire of the Celtic Tiger) have been loutishly lavished to the detriment of its ancient beauty. And yet, the spirit of rural Ireland does survive all around. Regularly I use a network of little roads on which one meets no more than three or four cars during a thirty-mile cycle through a landscape as exhilaratingly beautiful as any in the world. By following such roads, in Ireland's least developed corners, Christopher Somerville collected a series of authentic vignettes that emphasize what is distinctively Irish without entirely excluding the new 'globalized' Ireland. When he accompanied friends through a maze of boreens to buy flagons of poteen he noted a Japanese four-wheel-drive parked nearby – a vehicle no ordinary Irish farmer could have dreamed of possessing a mere decade ago.

Many newcomers to Ireland are disillusioned by our Celtic Tiger aspect but if they read this book, and give themselves time to follow in the author's footsteps, they can escape from that animal and may perhaps be inspired to contact the relevant authorities and plead with them to protect the beauty so memorably depicted and described in these pages.

Dervla Murphy

Chapter 1

WILL YOU COME IN?

'THAT'S THE WAY LIFE SHOULD BE,
THE DOOR NEVER CLOSED.'

Margaret Gallagher, Mullylusty, Co. Fermanagh

Margaret Gallagher and I have already been to Mass together this morning, sitting and kneeling side by side for an hour in the church down in Holywell village. But she still welcomes me across the threshold of her cottage at Mullylusty with a warm yet formal handshake, a sign that I am to consider myself a guest of honour while I am at her fireside.

The cottage is stone-built, floored with flagstones, whitewashed and thatched. It sits on a slope above Lough Macnean in south-west County Fermanagh, looking out to Belmore Mountain. You could spit from here across the border into the Irish Republic. Inside the house, a fire glows on the hearth. Margaret throws on a couple of sods of turf, and the fire sparks and throws out heat and a spicy smell that will linger in my sweater all day. Thick columns of smoke pour up the chimney over the blackened hooks and the kettle chain.

LEFT Under the thatch and over the step... Ireland's traditions of hospitality continue in many a rural cottage.

There is no electricity here, no running water. On this dull winter's morning the room is softy lit by the fire and by a slip of grey daylight through the little deep-set window. The chairs and dresser shine with a polish that is not sold in the supermarket – the patina of long use down the generations. The crockery is Belleek, valuable to those with an eye for what is old and good, valuable to Margaret because of its decades in the service of her family.

In her blue jeans and white sneakers Margaret bustles about, preparing tea. 'Living under thatch and over flags, as I do,' she throws over her shoulder as she reaches for the teapot, 'some visitors are surprised to find me dressed like this. They think I should be in a white embroidered apron and a little mob cap.' She brings home-baked brown bread and cakes to the hearth, and fills the teapot with water drawn from her well and boiled in the giant black kettle over the fire. We empty one pot after another while the talk skips by.

ABOVE Antique kitchen implements
that still make excellent tea and
goodies for the stranger.

RIGHT The country kitchen, a
stage for laughter, music, dancing
and endless tale-telling.

ABOVE Small farms like this one near
Ennis in Co. Clare are the backbone of
Irish rural life.

RIGHT Anne Kelly and Didi Korner of
Island More on their fishing boat in
Clew Bay, Co. Mayo.

'WELL, SO YOU'RE A
FRIEND OF CATHAL
McCONNELL'S ... SO NOW I'D
LIKE TO FIND
A TUNE FOR YOU.'

'Swedes, Yanks, Germans, Swiss, English, Japanese,' she says. 'They've all dropped in to see me. Yes, I make everyone welcome, because that's the way life should be, the door never closed. I don't keep my house like this, I don't live like this, to give tourists a folksy thrill, though. I do it for myself, because I love the life. I'm just continuing to live the way my parents and grandparents did, in the same house, in the same way.'

Margaret pours me a glass of whiskey and hands it carefully over. It is so full that only surface tension prevents the liquid from running down the outside of the glass. Margaret doesn't drink alcohol herself, but she loves to see its generous influence on people, the way it unzips them from shyness. I take the top off the drink and the bottle is immediately plied once more, to return the whiskey to a trembling convexity at the mouth of the glass. I consider my plans for the day, and reshuffle them lazily.

In her working life, Margaret co-ordinates training courses for unemployed people – 'that's me with a different hat on.' She has her hair fashionably tinted, drives a car, listens to modern music. She is no sackcloth-and-ashes anachronism, living out a plastic-

shamrock-and-leprechaun traditionalism. She lives this way because she loves it, and loves to draw strangers into it.

'Oh, I'm passionate about Fermanagh,' she tells me across the turf glow. 'The real Fermanagh, as I think of it – off the main roads, along the back lanes, out in the bog and on the mountain. I find the hand of God there in a hen harrier's wings, a cuckoo call or a flower.'

GUSSIE RUSSELL OF DOOLIN

The frame of the doorway between the kitchen and the pantry is where Gussie Russell finally comes to rest. I turned up an hour ago, unheralded, at the little roadside house above Doolin, armed with what in rural Ireland is an unrejectable calling card: the name of a mutual friend. Gussie, taken unawares while puzzling over the oily innards of a motorbike, shepherded me indoors. Since then he has been on the prowl from window to door, from table to cupboard, eyes shyly lowered, a gentle man considering the options of hospitality, unsure what to offer a stranger with as yet unstated requirements.

Now Gussie leans back against one wooden jamb and crosses his ankles, planting his boot soles on the base of the other, a serge-suited diagonal bisecting the hollow rectangle of the doorway. From a leather case he inches a scratched old tin whistle, and contemplates it in his palm. At last his eyes lift to meet mine for a moment. 'Well, so you're a friend of Cathal McConnell's ... So now I'd like to find a tune for you.' Silence returns, and lengthens. 'Well, Cathal would be fond of The Five Mile Chase,' murmurs Gussie, 'and so that's what I'll play for you.' He puts the whistle to his lips and flutters a little preliminary run of squeaky blips and pops, quarter-sounds that fall through the quiet of the room. Gussie nods to himself, settling more comfortably in the doorway. 'Will you tell Cathal when you see him next that I played you The Five Mile Chase?'

The tune curls round the kitchen, at first hesitant, then taking on speed and fluency, a running tune, a bridge between two strangers, a courtesy offered as proxy to a seldom-seen friend.

DIDI KORNER AND ANNE KELLY OF ISLAND MORE

The oars creak and chink gently in the rowlocks as Didi stretches back for another stroke. Over his shoulder Anne gives me a little smile, the kind of expression that says: 'Nearly there.' And over her shoulder I can see the house with its bird's-beak porch

PREVIOUS PAGE Inky shadows steal from the west over a rosy gold Clew Bay at sunset.

ABOVE The warm hospitality of the rural Irish is as traditional as their thatched cottages.

they have formed and forced with such careful labour from the walled garden on Island More.

Anne lights the paraffin lamps – there is no electricity on Island More. By their soft glow Didi and I make ready for a stroll about the island. We scramble up over the grassy ridges of long-erased field boundaries, treading a soft carpet of turf studded with orchids and clover. The nearby islets lie in the sunset like a shoal of hump-backed little sea monsters, their ink-black shadows spilling out across the unwrinkled silver of the bay. Due south across the water rises the dark cone head of Croagh Patrick, the holy mountain.

Down on the beach, idling back towards the house through the gathering night, we watch a big sea otter bound across the pebbles and slide into water as smooth as cream. All seems sweet and perfect, I remark to Didi. He laughs out loud. On the eighth or ninth day of a fortnight-long gale in winter, he says, when spray and sleet are sheeting horizontally in across the island, when the wind screams so loudly you feel it tearing at your mental stability, when the boat is about to drive ashore and smash to matchwood, when you would give any last thing in the world to be safe and snug in the pub on the far side of that bloody grey-faced bay – then things look a little different.

Back at the house we pull up our chairs to the table and set about demolishing a heap of vegetables that have just come out of the ground, and a mountain of baked oysters dredged from Clew Bay by Anne and Didi. Then we push back and light up, sipping home brew and watching the artichoke heads outside the window bob in the night breeze. 'Yes, there's times it feels like too much hard work,' says Anne, 'too cut off, just too difficult. But then there's times like tonight.' Didi nods, puffing away at his roll-up. 'I want to grow old on this island. I certainly intend to. We have what we need, and that's enough.'

HOSPITALITY, WEST LIMERICK

Sour blackberries and a peck of dust in the throat: they drive me off the hot back roads of west Limerick at last, and in through a stranger's gate in hopes of a glass of water. 'Well, come in,' invites the woman who answers my knock. 'You're welcome. Come on through to the kitchen. Leave your pack down. Would you like a cup of tea?'

Would I what? I drain my first cup standing up beside the kitchen table, my second sitting down. 'Thirsty, so you are,' smiles the woman, refilling. Her husband comes in from his gardening

crouched out of the path of the wind under a shoulder of hillside. The boat prow crunches into a shingly beach, and we clamber out. 'Welcome to Island More,' says Didi, shaking my hand as a grin splits his beard.

Last night in Westport, back there in Hoban's around midnight, Didi and Anne issued this invitation. Now, out here on Island More at the edge of things, with a rose and lemon sunset pouring in from the Atlantic across the hundreds of islets in Clew Bay, I find it hard to believe at all in that other, landward life. Can I really have known Didi and Anne for just three days? Here they are, their arms full of Westport-bought provisions, escorting me up the garden path with broad smiles as if I am some long-lost bosom friend, proudly pointing out the organic artichokes, the potatoes, beans and beetroots, the shallot patch and the broccoli bed that

LEFT AND BELOW 'Come in, now –
you'll have a cup of tea?' is a question
often asked of the foot-sore traveller in
Ireland. Not so much a question, in fact
– more a statement of intent.

and takes a seat opposite me. He, too, will have a cup of tea. In comes their daughter and her husband, the grandchildren, their friends. Someone scoots round the corner to the neighbours, to pass the word. The neighbours arrive and squash in. Now there are twenty people drinking tea in the little kitchen, the children fingering my pack, the dog sniffing my dusty boots. Everyone is friendly, shy, politely inquisitive. What is my name? Where have I walked from? And how far? Ten miles – in this heat? 'Yes, I thought you looked a bit – you know, red,' murmurs the woman. 'You'll have some of my new bread, now.'

A steaming brown loaf is put down, too hot to slice. We tear off chunks and eat them well buttered. A bottle of beer appears, inexpertly uncapped by a grandson, its foam collar lengthening till it drapes across the table. I drink, and tell my tale. Cross-currents of conversation eddy the attention away from me soon enough.

'So you're walking through Ireland,' muses the grandfather. 'What d'you think of the Irish, if you don't mind my asking?'

'Very hospitable,' I say. The old man is pleased. 'And you like our music? Wait, now, till I fetch the bodhrán.' He brings it to the table, a well-beaten shallow old drum, its goatskin shiny with battering. 'Will you sing us something?' I ask. His wife leans forward encouragingly. 'Oh, he used to be a great singer. Come on now, Tommy, won't you try one for us?' But Tommy comes over modest. He will – if I will first. There's no avoiding it, and anyway I have been hoarding a song which might slip into the mood without drawing down a show-stopping silence. So I push back my chair, tilt up my head and sing quietly what I can remember of 'The Flower of Magherally'.

'Your turn!' is the challenge to Tommy after I have done. But the old man demurs. Maybe he is too polite to outshine the stranger. No, he says, not now. But he will – he certainly will – when I come back to see them next year. We all understand this for a pleasant fiction. I sense it is time to ease the dog's head off my feet, stand up and don the pack once more. I shake hands all round and reel out into the road and on again between the dusty blackberry hedges, humming 'The Flower of Magherally' and tasting brown bread and bottled beer on each breath.

TINKERS, LETTERKENNY

The chrome-panelled caravans had arrived in Letterkenny during the night, and were drawn round in a defensive semi-circle under a low cliff at one side of the square. Elderly citizens went hurrying and hobbling in and out of St Eunan's Cathedral, but no-one

LEFT In many parts of rural Ireland the pony and trap is still a regular mode of transport.

BELOW RIGHT 'The cup o' tay, the cup o' tay, the finest sup 'twixt night and day'.

spared a glance across to the little alienated enclave. It was a sharp, windy morning in a cold spring, and people were glad to get in out of the chill.

The ground between and behind the caravans was already stained with sump oil and fire scorches, littered with greasy old car engines, rusted metal drums and bundles of rags. Under the caravans thin dogs quivered with tension and cold, too dispirited to raise a bark. From crooked tin chimneys trickles of smoke emerged, to be bent at right angles and streamed away by the wind. A rich smell pervaded the encampment: bonfire reek, turf smoke, damp earth, damp dog and cabbagey cooking smells.

A middle-aged man in a grubby vest, his lined bull's face under its brassy gold hair a mask of concentration, sat on the steps of one of the caravans with a piece of machinery wedged between his knees. He worked away at it with a screwdriver, entirely absorbed, immune to the cold. A youngish woman in down-at-heel slippers came slipping and slopping across from another caravan with a steaming mug in her hand, which she placed wordlessly on the step next to him. A yellowish lurcher dog with a sore nose crept out from under the caravan and came up to sniff at the mug. Without looking up from his work or changing the expression on his face, the man let out a roar so ferocious that the lurcher jumped as if it had been kicked and slunk away back under the van.

A crop-haired boy of about six looked out of the door to see what the row was about, and caught sight of me. Within a couple of seconds he was by my side, lifting a snotty face as he whined, 'Drop us a penny, mister?' I glanced down to see white worms of old scars crawling across his scalp. The man on the steps had looked up from his task and was watching. I patted my pockets; both empty. 'Sorry,' I said, with a sense of the feebleness of the word, and went on across the square. As I looked back from the steps of St Eunan's I caught a flicker of white from the caravan window – the twitch of lace as the boy's mother, who had also been watching in hopes of seeing the ploy bear fruit, let her curtain fall resignedly back across the steamy pane.

NUALA ENRIGHT OF SIXMILEBRIDGE

Nuala Enright pushed open the dining room door with her foot and came in with a laden tray. There was bingo tonight up at the GAA community hall at Sixmilebridge, unfinished business out in the kitchen, a suit of her husband's to sponge, and a hungry and footsore traveller with his chair pulled up to the table. No time for the elaborate display of cooking arts that she would have liked to bring out: 'just a plain country dinner,' as she said apologetically.

She twitched the cloth straight and put three dishes down on the table. In the first was a complete bacon ham. In the second, five floury potatoes out of the garden, their pale skins cracking. In the third, a pile of crinkly cabbage, dark green, steaming and smelling of iron.

The traveller thought that it was the best dinner he had eaten in three hundred miles.

BRACK FOR THE ARSE

Sitting back in a fold of heather, we collected our breath after the climb. The view over the heart of the Wicklow Hills was superb, reward enough for the 2,000ft upward slog. 'Lugnaquilla,' said

PREVIOUS PAGE Gazing on the Wicklow Hills: a view that hikers earn by the sweat of their brow.

ABOVE John McGing, pourer of the best pint of Guinness in Co. Mayo, behind his bar in Westport.

Derry, pointing across the valley. 'Hollow of the cocks, I believe it means.' Beside him, Conal glanced across the waterfalls of the Glenmacnass River and grinned. 'And our next hill is Tonelagee, which being interpreted meaneth Tóin le Gaoith – Arse in the Wind, I think the English would be.'

Derry rummaged in his pack. Black tea from an old Thermos, bitterly refreshing, and a solid slab of something wrapped in silver paper. 'Brack,' said Tricia, cutting a slice with her pocket knife. 'Home made. It'll cure you, or kill you.'

'BRACK,' SAID TRICIA, CUTTING A SLICE WITH HER POCKET KNIFE. 'HOME MADE. IT'LL CURE YOU, OR KILL YOU.'

Not nearly bread, not really pudding, not quite cake. Dark and delicious, moist and rich. Sultanas, cherries, lemon peel, nuts. Packed with everything bad for the waistline and good for the spirit; an unscientific, unbalanced jolt of ultra-sweet energy. We flew to the crest of the Arse, with the wind behind us all the way.

ULCER FRY

The traveller sat with his feet stretched well out under the table. The clock on the wall said nine, but he didn't necessarily believe that. His head rested on the back of his chair. Inside that head, last night's back bar dancers were performing a reprise in hobnail boots. There was a tremor in the left hand that had shaped guitar chords from seven o'clock in the evening until the lock-in had broken up with the dawn.

In front of him, an Ulster Fry: three rashers of bacon, two triangular slices of bread fried in bacon fat, four halves of fried tomato, a slice of fat-studded black pudding, a scoop of beans, a slice of bready white pudding, a spoonful of mushrooms and a wobbly fried egg. Also a pot of tea.

What can the dear B & B landlady have thought, after the traveller had paid his bill and walked off down the lane, when she came into the dining room to clear away and discovered an empty teapot and a full plate?

JOHN MCGING OF WESTPORT

Like a carpenter's collapsible rule, John McGing unfolds his lanky six-foot-something frame in stages. He rises in a series of right-

LEFT Some of rural Ireland's warmest hospitality is found under the sign of the B & B.

BELOW The beauties of Newport in Co. Mayo.

angles from his seat by the little iron stove at the top of the bar, where he sits out the cold winter afternoons. A year or so back it would have been Tot, the tiny and spherical pub dog, who reached the customer first with stiffly wagging tail. But Tot is now guardian of the great pub stove in the sky, and so it is John alone who greets the incomer.

John has the chart and substance of Westport's history in his head, and will deliver it to you – if he thinks you will be interested, and if he judges you to be a fit recipient of his facts and conjectures – in his quiet voice, salted and spiced with the

LEFT Behind the modest façade of McGing's bar in Westport lies one of Ireland's finest pubs.

RIGHT Small town produce fresh from the farm: an open-air cheese stall in Ennis, Co. Clare.

driest of quiet humour. He also pours the best pint of Guinness in County Mayo: a fighting statement, but a considered judgement. McGing's is a plain bar, plainly furnished. Its narrow wooden frontage says, simply, 'J.McGing'. John has hung the walls with cartoons of his friends, pictures and framed newspaper cuttings that he likes the look of, or thinks will chime well with the mood of his place. McGing's is essentially a talking pub, a place for conversation elliptical or sharp, punctuated with bursts of laughter, into which everyone is sooner or later drawn. It is a locals' place, a winter pub with a hot stove and an easy feel. Every now and then a bell pings at the street end of the pub, and there is a scuffling of feet as someone enters the tiny retail

section unseen beyond the wall. 'Ah,' says John behind the bar, lifting his head and one finger, 'there's a mouse in the trap.' And he goes down behind the wall to serve out a box of matches or a chocolate bar.

McGing's is where you will find Westport's session musicians – not playing, probably (though the impromptu sessions that do occasionally arise in John's pub are iconic in status and 'were-you-there?' value), but sipping stout, or red lemonade for those in a state of temporary realignment, as they contemplate late morning or mid-afternoon. Visitors, tourists, bodhrán thumpers and backpackers cram the renowned music pubs of Westport, hoping to see a hero or fall upon that fabulous item, the Mighty Session.

There are no heroes leaning on John McGing's bar, but this is where the lucky stumbler-in gets a glimpse of what that famous music, and that celebrated Irish crack, are really founded on.

HOME AND AWAY

Kate: 'Why? Well, I can't stay in Inishowen. Left school last year and I haven't had a job since. A bit of farm stuff, couple of weeks in a shop when they were short staffed. There's sod-all in Donegal. Not if you're young and got a bit of go in you, which I think I have. My da and ma both just went on the family farms when they were my age. But I can't. It's all gone back to bog, and you couldn't get any class of a living out of it. My uncles went to Liverpool and London in the construction, but I'm going to try and get over to Boston or New York, maybe the west. Take the fiddle, hope for the best. I might come back, but I don't think so. Haven't got a boyfriend or anything at the moment, haven't got

work to come back for. Don't want to just marry some Carndonagh boy I've known all my life, get pulled down with kids and that. There's nothing for me in Ireland, I'd say.'

Michael: 'Maybe. Maybe. Although in a way there wasn't any choice, because I'd a spot of trouble over there. I needed to get back to Ireland. Girl trouble, you know. Anyway, there's plenty of work now in Galway – around the city, all them new businesses with the European money. I might stay a year or two, look around a bit. But what I would really like to do is get back out to Skehanagh, out in East Galway, and take on the farm from the uncle that's in it now. He wrote me and said he wants me to come out, help him out. There's no living in it, a fifty-acre farm. But it's what my father would have liked, I think. It's what I want, a place that's mine, that I belong in, d'you know what I'm saying? The only place where any work I do will really mean something.'

Chapter 2

THE FAIR HILLS
OF IRELAND

'I WANTED TO KNOW: WHAT IS THAT PLANT,
THAT STONE, THAT PIECE OF ROCK?...
IT PUTS YOUR OWN MORTALITY INTO
PERSPECTIVE.' Tom Joyce, Slieve Bloom Hills, Co. Laois

LEFT Atlantic surges nibble endlessly at the rocks of Slea Head, Co. Kerry.

FOLLOWING PAGE Lough Feeagh lies at the feet of the Nephin Beg mountains in western Co. Mayo, one of Ireland's most remote spots.

Oliver Geraghty's grandfather must have been a very tough man. On market days he would rise in the dark and drive his cattle on foot from his farm near Newport in western County Mayo to the backwoods town of Bangor Erris, more than thirty miles to the north. Having sold his beasts to the dealer, and bought new ones, he would turn round and drive them all the way back to Newport. Sixty-four miles of walking: not on a well-surfaced road, but along a boggy crumbling track as wide as one cow's tread, that snaked and climbed through the heart of the Nephin Beg, the loneliest mountain wilderness in Ireland. When I came to walk the Bangor Trail with the drover's grandson, on a drizzling misty Sunday in May, I learned something of what it meant to cross 'the old and only pass into Erris'.

LEFT The leap and splash of Torc Waterfall near Killarney has enchanted visitors from Victorian times until the present.

ABOVE Tumbledown old houses, once refuges for drovers, dot the countryside of Connemara.

It took Oliver Geraghty and me twelve hours to cover the route. We had to ford the pebbled bed of the Tarsoghaunmore River barefoot, with our boots and socks in our hands. We passed the ruins of cottages where the drovers on the Bangor Trail might have hoped to get a bite to eat. We climbed the shoulders of mountains whose pale quartzite peaks stood hidden in the mist 2,000ft overhead, and dropped into silent valleys full of sedge and bog. We drank cold, sweet water in our cupped hands from peat-brown waterfalls. Often the rotten surface of the track gave way, sucking our legs down to the knee, necessitating a squelching struggle to get free. We stumbled on grass tussocks, skidded on stones, sat down in bog pools and mud holes.

I limped down the road into Newport a very tired man, smeared with peat stains, soaked in sweat, rain and mist, both boots spouting bog water at every step, glowing with that end-of-a-long-day satisfaction that every long-distance walker knows. For me it had been, comparatively, an easy ride. I had made the crossing of the Nephin Beg in the cheerful company of Oliver, trusting to his expert direction-finding. I was dressed in the latest waterproof gear and shod with lightweight modern hiking boots; I had hot coffee in a Thermos flask, chocolate bars, sandwiches, energy tablets if I needed them. I had walked for the fun of it, too, for the pleasure of overcoming bad ground and bad weather.

Sitting back in a Newport pub that night with a pint of Guinness in front of me and a good dinner under my belt, I thought of the old man and his struggle to make a living, the hard life of the small Mayo farm that drove him out alone through the bogs and over the mountains, worrying and chivvying his cattle as they strayed, far from help should he break a leg or get stuck in a bog, hurrying to avoid being caught out at night on the track. A tough road indeed, those sixty-four miles beaten out in hobnail boots under the spur of hunger and hard times.

HARD LIFE ON THE BLASKET

A house on a hillside in western Kerry, looking out to the green hump of Great Blasket Island two miles across the white tide-rips of Blasket Sound. Across his turf fire Seán O'Catháin speaks, slowly, feeling for the English words that are still unfamiliar on

his tongue. He came ashore at the age of forty, in 1953, when the few remaining islanders decided to evacuate the Blasket.

'Well, it was a hard life, that time, out on the Blasket. Ten children in one room. We were poor. Everything was carried on the back. The currach, too – very heavy. But we were strong. We would row the currach thirteen miles out to the Tearacht and back again, to climb the cliffs and gather seagulls' eggs. Have you never tried one? They're good!

'We ate potatoes and fish, and puffins. Everyone had one cow. We had to put them in the currach to bring them to the bull on the mainland. Their legs were tied. How they used to struggle! It was very dangerous, rowing across the Sound. We would sell mackerel and lobster in Dingle, nine shillings a dozen for lobsters. You have to pay five pounds for one now!

'We had to leave, you see. All the girls went to the mainland. It's a better life here, anyway, on dry land. There are only a few of us islanders left now, all Gaelic speakers, and all getting old. I don't miss the island at all. It was very, very hard.'

THE FEEL OF SLIEVE BLOOM

The Slieve Bloom mountains rise in a heathery dome from the flat plains of the midlands where Tipperary moves over into Laois. A wonderful splashy footpath rings their heights, all but unwalked. Views are huge, winds cold, the ground underfoot of rock and bog, heather and grass. When Tom Joyce walks Slieve Bloom, he does so with one hand trailing to savour the feel of heather tops, bog plants and rock lichens.

'I began exploring these hills when I was a youngster. I'd have eight ounces of lunch and two stone of books on my back. I wanted to know: what is that plant, that stone, that piece of rock? When you dig your hands into this peat, reaching down 5,000 years, it puts your own mortality into perspective. I found out that the Slieve Blooms were as high as the Himalayas a couple of million years ago. Before that they'd been a flat flood plain. The power of natural forces, dramatic like a great volcanic upheaval or amazingly slow like the drip of rain on rock – it makes you think.'

LEFT On the Dingle peninsula
you can still meet men and women
who were born and bred   RIGHT Looking from Slea Head
on the Blasket Islands.   towards the hump of Great
                                 Blasket Island.

THE HAUNT OF WILD GEESE

We landed on a tiny slip of island from a rubber boat on a miraculously swell-free day. We found an early medieval church there, with an altar of fantastically coloured stones and a cramped chamber where repentant prodigals would fold themselves away

LEFT The wild Kerry coastline around Slea Head is rugged and storm-bitten.

BELOW The large, papery blooms of the yellow iris or flag, beautifying wet fields and bogland all over Ireland.

to purge their sins through gross bodily discomfort. On the altar, a bevelled stone sanctuary lamp fifteen hundred years old. Encircling the church, the Stations of the Cross: a ring of standing stones cut into blunt-armed crosses well over a thousand years old. Some were carved with faces. Offerings of white quartz and bright flowers had been laid before the stones; the flowers were fresh, picked that day or the day before. Over all, a profound nerve-tingling stillness.

'The haunt of wild geese' was all that the writer of my guidebook had found to say about this wholly magical place. Or had he, too, understood that magic divulged is magic no more?

TALKING THE WALKING

The hill roads and tracks of the south-west, where Kerry and Cork shoulder each other. Between Kenmare and Bantry a rising and falling land, never quite lifting into mountains, for ever putting a hill in your way and replacing it with a valley. There are grand mountains to the north in the Ring of Kerry, and steep country to the west along the spine of Beara; but the old drove roads south into Cork take clever short cuts through narrow passes and over the backs of the hills, always finding the easiest way through. Jack Buckley of Cork walks this landscape – great marathon walks, dozens of miles together at four miles an hour, his wiry elderly body as keen as a whippet, his arms pumping, as statistics, stories, claims, facts and fancies spill out of his mouth.

'... up and around Coolnacoppagh and Curragrainue, that might have the meaning of the bog or maybe the hollow where Gráinne slept with Diarmuid, you know, the star-crossed lovers. So then we'd be a short mile or two up to Drehideighteragh, which I couldn't put a meaning to, but anyway from there it's only a step up to the Priest's Lep at the top of the pass where you'll get a grand view out and down into Bantry Bay and across Whiddy Island where they had that terrible disaster of a tanker at the oil jetty there, a roar you could hear fifteen miles off, *Betelgeuse*, I think she was called. So anyway, as I was telling you, we'd a walk planned from Cork to Limerick, now that's sixty miles and so a

'I BEGAN EXPLORING THESE HILLS WHEN I WAS A YOUNGSTER. I'D HAVE EIGHT OUNCES OF LUNCH AND TWO STONE OF BOOKS ON MY BACK.'

friend of mine and myself had a little walk of thirty-eight miles to prepare for it, but your man turned up late and we didn't get away till half-past six in the morning. Well, I'd telephoned a pub out the road to have a meal ready for us the way we wouldn't waste any time on having to order it, but didn't the waitress come round and ask us what we'd like to eat, God save us! Jakers, says I, sure we'll never get away! But anyway we get out and on our way, and came in past midnight so we missed out on the check-in, but at least we'd done it under the twenty-four hours all right ...'

THE BURREN AND MARYANGELA

'Now if I'd washed my face in the dew on a clump of those this
morning,' says Maryangela Keane, pointing to a sprig of eyebright,
'I'd have a pair of gorgeous bright eyes to bedazzle you with.' She
laughs, throwing her hair back like a young girl in spite of her

ABOVE Stone walls built laboriously
by hand are characteristic of the open
landscapes of Co. Kerry.

seventy-five years, as she tips back on her heels on the naked warm pavement of the Burren. When you come botanising in early summer in North Clare's Burren region, that strange grey world of stepped limestone hills, you need someone like Maryangela by your side, someone knowledgeable, inquisitive, humorous and entirely in love with this haunting landscape.

The Burren is the most magical place in County Clare, 500 square miles of round hills and coastal flatlands bedded on limestone pavement warmed by the sun and the Gulf Stream. Nearly 300 million years ago the Burren was a flat seabed. Then it rose, bulging upwards until the limestone surface cracked across like the bark of an ilex tree. Those cracks remain, narrow fissures up to five feet deep that geologists call 'grykes', in which grow an incredible flora. 'You see,' explains Maryangela, fingering the creamy cup-shaped blooms of mountain avens, 'it was probably

ABOVE A stunning flora flourishes in the limestone cracks of the Burren to puzzle and intrigue botanists.

RIGHT The weatherworn geology of the Burren produces a landscape of fissured rock pavements.

FAR RIGHT Five thousand years ago the late Stone Age tomb architects raised this dolmen at Poulabrone in the heart of the Burren.

the glaciers of the Ice Age that brought arctic and alpine plants like this one down here as seeds, and left them behind when they melted. But we don't really know exactly why you'll get them thriving alongside plants like that' – she points to a straggle of hoary rockrose – 'which is a real southerner. Also it's a puzzle how you'll get heather, which loves acid soils, and milkwort, which can only thrive on lime, growing quite happily side by side. Something to do with the right proportions of warmth, shade and sunlight – and rain, of course, which we do have rather a lot of.'

The Burren is full of mystery. Strange lakes called turloughs empty and fill as if by magic. Plants of the high places such as mountain saxifrage grow down by the sea. Ivies and violets normally found only in woodland thrive in a landscape that is all but treeless. Remains of ancient settlements, monastic and domestic, lie scattered across the riverless, naked, unaccommodating hills. Nowadays people live around the

perimeter of the Burren, in close-knit villages where the music and gossip are fierce. You can lose your heart to the Burren, as easy as winking, an expatriate Clareman once said to me; a true word.

BONES OF OMEY ISLAND

It may be sea, or it may be sand: the way you cross over from Claddaghduff to Omey Island depends on the tide and the state of Connemara's wind and weather. Everything blows wild from time to time out here in the western tip of County Galway. But given a fine day and a low tide you can cross the sands on foot in ten minutes.

Omey Island lies low, like most of the other islands and islets scattered in the sea off Connemara. Omey is founded on granite, topped with lush flowery grass bedded on a thick layer of sand and fragments of lime-rich shells blown here by the Atlantic wind. There are complete shells in the sandy layer, too: shells of cockle and limpet, along with crumbly chunks of granite reddened in long-ago cooking fires. These couple of miles of tidal island are home to perhaps a dozen people today, but a thousand years ago there might have been ten or twenty times that number, subsisting on boiled shellfish and whatever else happened their way. The ruins of their dwellings, stone-walled and ash-floored, are exposed along the sand cliffs after winter storms.

It is not only shells that enrich the turf of Omey. The rabbits that infest the island throw out human bones from their burrows – a femur, a scapula, part of a skull. Omey Island has been holy ground ever since St Feichín established a monastery here in the mid-seventh century; maybe long before that, too, since early Christian hermits tended, wisely, to pick sites that already had spiritual significance for the local people. Who knows how many thousand dead, over how many thousands of years, have been brought across the sands or rowed over to Omey to be buried along with their ancestors? The custom continues to this day.

RIGHT Storm clouds gather over the Atlantic ocean, to come racing in over Omey Island.

TOP LEFT Believers leave tokens in hopes of a cure at St Feichín's Well on Omey Island, Connemara.

FERRYING HER OVER

They are ferrying her over from Claddaghduff,
the schoolteacher's mother, in suitable weather:
grey, wild, wintry.
                    Salt wood
faces clench round cigarettes,
quiet jokes crack in cars creeping
across the sands to Omey Island.

A plain way of death, these
ritual lines drawn in sand
down long time, binding
shore to island. Stones mark them,
and the shared cup.
                    The low cliffs yield

shards of a wise woman's cranium,
saint's patella, fisherman's scapula:
worked out.

                    She's quickly shouldered
up from the hearse, swayed high. Tobacco
breath comes short, black suits flap.
They launch her as they would a currach.

Storms rake the cliffs, mix old bones
with shell and sand. Orchids thrive on
Omey's rich sward.
                    Nothing has changed.
They'll drink to her in Sweeney's, then
let the dark island have her.

TIM ROBINSON LIFTS THE VEIL

'OMEY ISLAND/IOMAIDH, anciently Iomaidh Feichín/St Feichín's
bed or seat.' Thus Tim Robinson, in his 'Folding Landscape'
Gazetteer of Connemara, lifts the veil a little for those who do not
speak Gaelic. 'If you don't have the Gaelic you'll travel through
Ireland like a blind and deaf man,' is a saying worthy to be noted.
Precious few of Her Britannic Majesty Queen Victoria's sappers had
the Gaelic, and they and others who wrenched the meaningful Irish
into meaningless transliterated Anglo-nonsense wiped both the
practical signposts and the poetry of an oral geography clean off the
maps even as they surveyed and drew them up.

Tim Robinson, an Englishman who has lived in Connemara
since 1972, has the Gaelic, and a passion for the West of Ireland
that has led him to map its shores and hills with a matchless
precision and understanding. 'When I walk the land of
Connemara,' he says, 'it's as if my pen is moving over the paper;
and when I'm drawing the maps, to me it's as if I'm walking across
the land.' The spidery, hand-drawn 'Folding Landscapes' of
Connemara, the Aran Islands and the Burren that he has published
from his studio in Roundstone, County Galway, are works of art,
and treasures of reference. Every field, shore, rock and dwelling
has its Irish name, and every name has meaning: descriptive, or
historical, humorous, or springing from legend. To wander with a

OPPOSITE LEFT Seabirds find
undisturbed roosts in the crags of
Ireland's remote sea cliffs.

ABOVE Tim Robinson, gazetteer of
Connemara, unlocks another Folding
Landscape (detail BELOW LEFT).

'Folding Landscape' in hand is like having a fluent and sympathetic
interpreter whispering in your ear as you listen in on a
conversation in an unknown tongue. It draws back the curtain on
views out across another, hitherto hidden country, one that fits as
close as skin beside the outward and visible landscape: a country
whose riches remain locked away until Gaelic turns the key.

Picture the islanders of Inishshark naming their coves and
cliffs, each with its natural asset so vital to their difficult and
precarious existence eight miles offshore: Fó na gColm, the cove
of the rock doves; Aill na nUibheacha, the cliff of the eggs; Fó na
Móna, the cove of the turf; Fó Duilisc, the cove of the dulse or
edible seaweed. Consider the expressiveness of Bun Dúghlaise,
the black stream foot, for a place where a stream flows over the
blackened stumps of ancient pine trees on the beach. Rendered
'Bundouglas' in English, it loses all sense.

How brilliantly these clumsy Anglo place names play on
the imagination, once the sheen of Gaelic meaning is brought to
the surface:

- Shanakeever – Seanadh Chíamhair, the gloomy slope
- Gooreenatinny – Guairín an tSionnaigh, the fox's small sandbank
- Tooraskeheen – Tuar an Sceichín, the bleaching green with the small thorn tree
- Roundstone – Cloch na Rón, the stone of the seals
- Rusheenyvulligan – Roisín an Bholgáin, the small peninsula of the swelling
- Glenagevla – Gleann na nGeimhleach, the glen of the fetters or captives
- Derreenagusfoor – Doirín na gCos Fuar, the small wood of the cold feet (all that was left of a herdsman eaten by a bull in the wood, according to local lore)
- Muckinishederdauhaulia – Muiceanach Idir dhá Sháile, the pig-shaped hill between two salt waters

GEESE OF STRANGFORD LOUGH

A cold autumn day on Strangford Lough, with a blasting wind cutting up from the Irish Sea across County Down. The low-lying barrier of the Ards Peninsula, hanging southwards like an arm from a shoulder of coast to the east of Belfast, is no protection: the

LEFT Fierce Mayo seas whipped up by storm winds pound the shores of Achill Island.

BELOW Brent geese feed peacefully on eel-grass on the muddy shores of Strangford Lough, Co. Down.

20-mile-long sea lough that it cradles is wide open to this south-easterly gale. Trees thrash wildly, seaweed hanks bowl like tumbleweed up the muddy shores, and the slowly rising water in the tidal lough is ribbed across with long wind streaks.

The light-bellied brent geese, 12,000 of them, arrived from Greenland a week or so ago for their annual winter stay on Strangford Lough. Now they are fighting this big wind – or rather, as I see when I look more closely, they are surfing down its invisible tube, balancing delicately a couple of feet above the mud, with shivering wings feeling for holds in the pulsating streams of air, feet extended in front of them, the black webs at full stretch. They make their landing approach cautiously, backing their feathers against the gale until gravity overcomes the stalling speed and they plop down onto the mud with a tiny splash. The small heads dip forward like sprinters competing for the finishing tape, then straighten; the wings are shivered and shaken like wet umbrellas before being tucked neatly back in a round-elbowed fold. The heads on their stalk-like dark necks, each with its clean white parsonical collar, are held high in deep suspicion for half a minute as the brents sweep their surroundings through a ninety-degree swivel of each eye. Then the heads are given a slight shake, the geese waddle forward and lower their beaks to the mist-like thickets of zostera marina that seethe in the wind endlessly raking the lough shore.

SEA OF TALES

Another brisk day, this one a late spring morning on the Atlantic-facing coast of Sligo. Flocks of knot are skimming with the wind over Dunmoran Strand, flickering above their own reflections in the mirror gleam of the sands. Low cliffs tufted with wind-shaken

LEFT A thatched house on Inishmore in the Aran Islands: a deeply traditional way of life on the verge of extinction.

BELOW LEFT 'Stone walls stripe the Aran Islands… in a balanced and intimate geometry that lets light pass between each individual stone.'

clumps of thrift hold a couple of ruined farmhouses whose walls sprout a pale green stubble of lichen. The wind runs through heather, grass and pink thrift clumps. The sands have been silvered by the falling tide, and above them the bellies of dark racing clouds shine with a thick silvery light.

I climb from Dunmoran Strand to cross the cliffs at Lenadoon Point, and stand there to taste a last view back east. The concave war-galley prow of Benbulben stands out tiny but sharp across Sligo Bay. The mythical hero Diarmuid was killed on its slopes in a frantic chase. Was it a wild boar who pierced his Achilles heel, or was it the Fianna, the warrior host of the jealous Fionn MacCumhaill, who hunted him to death? There is button-topped Knocknarea, too, where Queen Mebh of Connacht lies buried. After a boasting contest with her husband King Ailill she raided Ulster to capture the Great Brown Bull of Cooley, and almost met her death at the sword-point of the mighty Ulsterman hero Cuchulainn when she ill-advisedly stopped to pass water in the heart of battle.

I have heard these tales, and read them in books and in Yeats's poems, while walking through Sligo. Now I swing round, climb down and head out west into County Mayo and a fresh sea of tales.

WALLS OF ARAN

The three Aran islands swim in line astern, from the coast of County Clare out into Galway Bay. Long-backed Inishmore heads the convoy, the wedge of Inishmaan rises in the middle of the group, and little leaf-shaped Inisheer brings up the rear. Administratively the Aran Islands belong to granite-scabbed south Galway; geologically they are pure Clare limestone. Culturally and atmospherically they tend to be themselves, three discrete pieces that form a land apart.

Their landscape is astonishing, three dark deserts of smoothed naked rock that only slowly reveal their secrets – standing stones, ancient churches that seem to have grown out of the limestone pavement, square cliffs dropping to great caves, brilliant spring flowers crouched in cracks and hollows, Iron Age forts of curving defensive design that hold to the clifftops, braced for some forgotten blow from the open sea.

Stone walls stripe the islands, aligned north to south as if raked straight by the comb of a fastidious giant. They mark out the boundaries of pastures so rocky that cattle and sheep can hardly find grazing among the limestone slabs, and of tiny vegetable fields whose furrowed soil has been laboriously created by hand from seaweed and sand. The walls snake with the island roads, rough-surfaced boreens for the most part where a bicycle or pair of feet are more use than a motor car. There are precious few cars on the islands.

These workaday yet ornate walls are made of thin blades of limestone, painstakingly cleared by hand from the fields and piled together in a balanced and intimate geometry that lets light pass

between each individual stone. On a sparkling bright day, sea and sky come through the black lacework of the wall in a jigsaw of coloured fragments like the stained glass windows of some open-air cathedral.

OUT THE BOG

When an English mouth says 'bog', there's a dismissive air to the short, sharp syllable, the sound of a door shutting on every quality but squelch and stink. 'Bog' sounds faecal, mucky, a slough of waste matter. In an Irish mouth – the more rural the better – the word softens and lengthens, filling out richly. 'I'm going out the bog, cutting a bit of turf,' a West Limerick farmer shouts in my ear as he gives me a ride on the towbar of his noisy tractor. ''Tis a very peaceful place to be, the baw-oo-gh,' and he draws out the word into two, perhaps three separate syllables. 'You can really wind down and be easy out there.'

On a bog road in southern Connemara, backpack dumped on the grass verge, hands in pockets, I idle and watch others work. It is a blazing hot summer's afternoon, and the sun strikes brilliant glints out of bog pools iridescent with mineral slicks. The heat draws a rich, fruity smell out of the heather and grass, and causes seed pods to tick like malfunctioning clocks as they burst. The bog stretches away, brown and green, its shaggy skin pierced by countless bone-white outcrops of granite. The blue profile of the Maumturk Mountains, a magnificent backdrop, heaves like a stormy sea on the northern horizon.

Perhaps forty people are at work in this landscape, though dotted at such remove from each other that I can only spot five or six with my sun-dazzled eyes. Michael, a red-haired man in a shiny acrylic teeshirt, is driving a slim blade on a wooden handle into the soft depths of his turf bank with a shove of his boot. This morning he has already cut a couple of hundred rectangular sods of turf, each eighteen inches long, and laid them out to dry in chocolate-brown rows on the grass. The open turf face from which he has quarried them, seven sods wide, is steadily retreating under the depredations of the blade. By the time Michael stops to eat his sandwiches, he will have cut nearly a week's fuel for the fire and left a neat pit in the bog about the size of a double grave.

Michael's eleven-year-old son – who certainly ought to be in school today – is collecting crisp dried sods of turf that his father cut a few days ago. When he has a wheelbarrow full he trundles them across the bog to the road near where I am lounging. His mother and another man, one of Michael's brothers to judge by his red hair and similarly stocky build, unpack the barrow and add the sods to the family's hump-backed miniature hillock of turf. When everything is properly dry, someone's tractor and trailer will transport the fuel to the family house in Kilbrickan or Rosmuc.

The bog has been laid down over the past seven or eight thousand years, a tangle of vegetable roots and leaves unable to rot thanks to the acidic nature of the underlying rock. Harvested by hand and with traditional tools and methods, as Michael and his family have been doing, the rate of attrition is so slow as to be virtually negligible.

'Come here,' says Pat Dooley of Bord na Móna, the Irish Peat Board. 'Do you see this piece of bog oak?' We are at the bottom of an iron staircase, thirty feet down inside the moist body of the Blackwater Bog in the north-west corner of County Offaly. 'This bit of wood is probably 6,000 years old – the tree must have been growing here literally thousands of years before the Pharaohs ever thought of building their pyramids in Egypt.' The bog oak is delicately grooved, subtly striated, more like a section through a piece of muscle than a chunk of prehistoric wood.

Up at the surface of the Blackwater Bog, destruction and ruin stretch to the flat horizon. Open-cast peat-cutting machines rip off the green top blanket of the bog and churn their way through the upper layers, tearing out the peat to be milled into dust for industrial fuel or chopped into briquettes for domestic burning. What the machines leave behind when they move on is a raw black wasteland of muddy, waterlogged, devastated ground uncannily like some First World War battlefield in Flanders.

One-seventh of Ireland's total land mass is peat bog. In a coal-less country with precious few forests, peat (known as 'turf' in Ireland) is a highly desirable commodity. You can generate electricity by burning it in a power station. It is a great purifier, a cradle for the nurturing and growth of plants, an emollient of skin afflictions, and a fragrant source of light and heat when burned in a domestic fireplace. Since Bord na Móna came into being in 1946 with a brief to 'develop' the bogs with sophisticated machinery,

hundreds of miles of bog have been cut to ribbons and left as black, waterlogged morasses. It is a national scandal, a wholesale vandalism.

Now, with Ireland's commercially viable peat reserves due to be worked out in the not too distant future, Bord na Móna is trying to do something about the devastation it has wrought. The board owns around 200,000 acres of bog. If things go according to plan, Bord na Móna will become a highly influential player in the conservation stakes. The idea is to reclaim the peat lands and convert them into a mosaic of wetlands, lakes, fens, forests and nature reserves. It will not cancel the destruction of the past half-century. What it will do is to create a refuge for wildlife, and put a brake on future commercial development of the bogland.

Thirty years ago, only poets and naturalists went to the bog for pleasure. Thirty years hence, the transformed industrial bogs may well become one of Ireland's top leisure attractions.

TOP LEFT Saving the turf demands hard sweated labour, with the whole family having to lend a hand.

RIGHT Connemara bogland: wide and mysterious, a place to wind down and be easy.

Chapter 3

THE BONNY LABOURING BOY

'I WOULDN'T DO ANYTHING ELSE
FOR A LIVING. THE EEL FISHING'S
IN MY BLOOD, YOU SEE.' **Christy, Lough Neagh Fisherman, Co. Tyrone**

A good strong north-west wind is blowing across County Tyrone, rattling the loose rails and doors of the sheep pens at Forbes's Mart on the outskirts of the little market town of Castlederg. Inside the plain building, a circle of flat cloth caps and greasy billycock hats rims the auction ring. Some of these hill-farming faces are hard, some humorous. All are intent on the sheep that come jostling and bumping nervously in through the iron gate. A three-year-old boy stands up on the topmost rail, rigid with delight at being so close to the sheep, one hand twined in his father's curly grey hair. Two balding, red-cheeked bachelor brothers, identical twins, sit side by side on the cold concrete steps, their big knobbed hands folded in their laps. One scratches his left ear, the other his right: an image some smart character photographer would die for, if one were present in this chilly, dark barn of a building.

LEFT Saving the hay: the traditional farming methods still in use in rural Ireland often mean long hours of hard labour for small gain.

'Thirty-one, thirty-one, thirty-one,' intones the auctioneer in a rapid-fire jabber. His eyes pinball over the ring of farmers. A pair of fingers flicks upwards. 'Thirty-one-twenty, Jim. Thirty-one-twenty, thirty-one-twenty, thirty-one-twenty...' Smack! goes the auctioneer's stick on his little counter. 'Sold to Jim Doyle.' No flicker of expression on the purchaser's face as the gate clangs behind his ten new lambs. He does not give them a glance, but continues to whisper secretively into his neighbour's ear, part of a mysterious insider's ritual.

SAVING THE HAY

With a long-handled rake the old woman turns over the cut grass, paled to a colour nearer white than green after a month of hot rainless days on the Dingle peninsula. The hay meadow, a rough rectangle bounded by stone walls, measures perhaps thirty feet by thirty, the dimensions of a good-sized drawing room in one of Dublin's Georgian houses. Out here in western County Kerry, the contents of the tiny field and its couple of neighbouring meadows are so central to the winter economy of this woman's ten-cow farm that it is worth her while to invest several days of the hottest summer anyone can remember in manual labour that would ache a back forty years younger than hers.

When the cut grass is dry she forks it up into a number of waist-high, beehive-shaped haycocks. Each cock is capped with a

BELOW The Ring – intent purchasers watch for every minute flaw in the beasts for sale.

RIGHT Slow rhythms, slow progress: the homeward amble of cows at milking time.

square of rain-proof tarpaulin, held down against the wind by a fringe of ropes weighted with dangling beach stones. The little gathering of haycocks, a dozen to each of the three meadows, takes stance over a day or two, looking like a colony of strange fungi. 'Instead of feeding this stuff to the cows,' grunts the farmer's city-born grandson, jacket off and hayfork in hand, in a wry aside across the field wall, 'she should be charging the tourists ten pound every time they stop to take a photograph. That'd soon buy her a retirement ticket to the Bahamas ...'

EELS IN THE BLOOD

The yellow oilskins, slickly gleaming in the light of a lantern, creak as Christy bends and straightens, bends and straightens. Beyond him at the bulwarks of the open boat, the dimly seen figure of his partner Martin dips and rises rhythmically. The arms of both young men swing back and forth like pistons as the long net is hauled up from the silky dark water of Lough Neagh and brought dripping inboard, yard by yard.

It is the last draft of the night. Ten eels coil wetly in the folds of the net, thrashing as Christy disentangles them one by one and slips them into a plastic barrel of lake water. 'A poor night,' he murmurs. 'But you have to look on the bright side. My wife could have been a widow if we'd upset the boat, so things aren't as bad as they might have been.'

Rope and nets are neatly coiled at the side of the boat. Occasionally a faint splash comes from the barrel where a couple of dozen eels are writhing. Christy and Martin light cigarettes. Overhead the sky shimmers with stars, but a quiet breeze has blurred their reflection in Lough Neagh.

'Except for the nylon of the net,' says Christy, 'nothing at all has changed with this eel fishing for hundreds of years. I like to think of that. Maybe it's been a poor night tonight, but there'll be better ones. I wouldn't do anything else for a living. The eel fishing's in my blood, you see.'

LEAVING THE FARM

It had been a long, long day's hike in the hills of Donegal. Now the wind and rain were at my back, shoving me the last couple of miles like a pair of bullies whose worst was nearly done. The farm, when I came across it in the half-light of evening, looked

overwhelmed with rainwater. Cows stood in a boggy slough round a hay manger in the middle of a field, smeared with mud from nose to tail, shifting from side to side with that monumental patience of cattle as they dragged their sinking legs one by one out of belly-deep mire. The wet land was shaggy with thistles. The field walls were tumbledown. It looked as if all care and pride in the place had washed away with the rain.

In front of me the farmer and his wife were splashing down the lane, prodding half a dozen cows ahead of them through the puddles. 'Hiking, are ye?' said the man, sardonically, as I caught up with them. 'Well, ye've picked the wrong evening for it!' In the gateway of their farmyard they stopped for a chat as the rain let up.

'Well, we can just squeeze out a living from the farm. But we've only thirty acres, and the land is terrible stony and full of bog. I suppose us old ones can make do on what our fathers made do on. My father, who had this farm before me, now he wouldn't go into Letterkenny to the shops from one month's end to the next. Only the market would draw him into the town, ye see, so he hadn't a need for more than a few pounds of money. And

LEFT Waiting for the next catch: a fishing boat moored in a sheltered corner of Roundstone Bay, Co. Galway.

ABOVE Beauty and usefulness combined in the patterns of these fishing nets on a jetty in Co. Cork.

'MY WIFE COULD HAVE BEEN A WIDOW IF WE'D UPSET THE BOAT, SO THINGS AREN'T AS BAD AS THEY MIGHT HAVE BEEN.'

we've been content with the same kind of living out of this farm, with our own milk and eggs and vegetables, for all the years we have been married. But we're not getting any younger, and we don't get the government grants like we used to. It has ye losing heart, doesn't it?

'Our children? Oh, they're away from this. We've one boy over in America as a sound man for the big bands, and another working in a recording studio away down in Dublin. And the girl's a radiographer. All making better livings than I could ever have dreamed about at their age. Better livings than they can get here, anyway. Sure they wouldn't want to stay on the farm at all. It'll all go when we do.'

PEG DOWN THE CURRACH

A wild day on Inishmaan, with a storm brewing out in Galway Bay. Down on the slipway in the shelter of the island's pier, two men in oilskins are preparing their currach hastily for a brief trip to pull up their lobster pots before the weather worsens. The long black-hulled canoe, stored upside down when not in use, has been turned right way up and set ready in a small wheeled cradle on

ABOVE The main source of livelihood for many of Ireland's farmers: cows returning to their farm in Co. Clare.

RIGHT The distinctive shape of the currach revealed as it is set to dry on land.

the ribbed concrete slip. She is eighteen feet long and about three wide, wooden-framed with a tarred canvas skin, tapering to a sharp uptilted prow. Her square transom holds a small outboard engine. She is no quaint museum piece, but a practical tool for getting a living in the harsh, unforgiving environment of the Aran Islands. Currachs are great sea boats, say the islanders, extremely responsive to waves and wind, delicate to handle and surprisingly strong. In a lively sea they also ship a lot of water and leap about like bucking broncos.

Now the two fishermen are ready to set off. One takes his place in the currach and grasps the oars. His partner lifts the end of the cradle, waits for a higher wave than hitherto, and walks cradle and boat forward into the water. The oars sweep vigorously back and forth, and the black shark shape of the currach slides out of the cradle and floats free. The steersman runs the cradle a little way back up the ramp, while the rower steadies the currach. In hops the

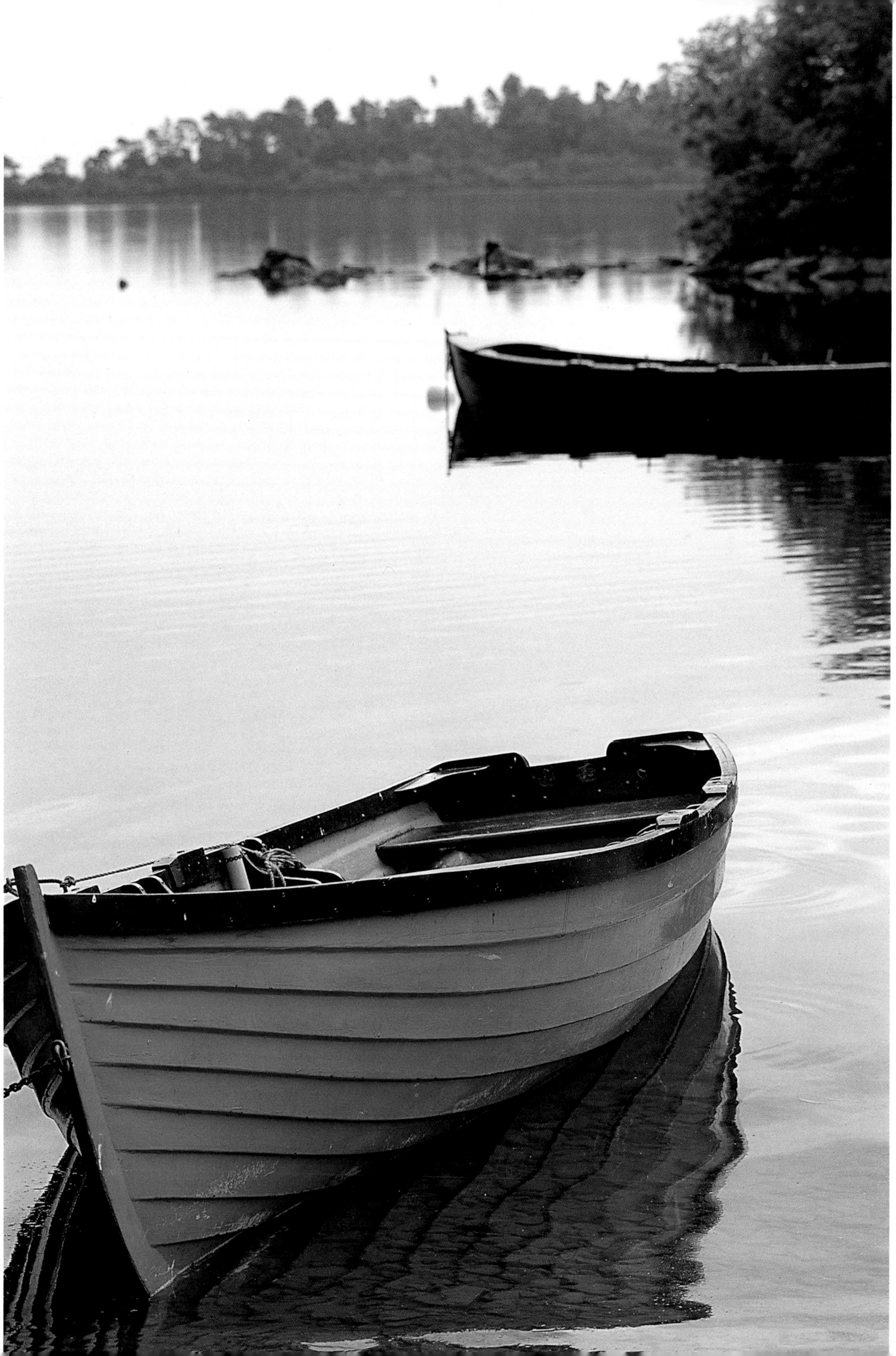

steersman; he pulls the lanyard, the outboard motor coughs and roars, the oars are shipped, and the currach motors off north around the coast, tossing her head as she shakes water and spray aside. By the time she reappears the wind and sea have both risen, and waves are beginning to thump whitely along the shore. The tide has risen too, enabling the steersman to bring the currach skilfully in over the top of the slipway, where he jumps out and runs for the wheeled cradle with the waves at his heels. With the currach safely beached, a dozen pots are lifted out. The oarsman shows me the catch: one small lobster, its jointed armour a rich navy blue.

The fishermen turn the currach upside down and spread a net over her, pegging down the edges. It is going to be quite a storm – one that will last three days, as things turn out. They have had to pull up their pots far too early, and have a wasted setting expedition to rue. But other Inishmaan fishermen have gambled on the storm being short and not too severe, and have left their pots in position on the seabed. They will regret their decision in the morning when they discover such of their pots as can still be found, flung far inland by the power of unleashed waves and wind.

'DRUM HARDER – LIVE LONGER! WALLUP!'

'Now when we started out in Roundstone,' says Malachy 'Bodhrán' Kearns, 'we didn't even have a telephone that worked. Here I was, a refugee from a high-pressure job in Dublin, you know, trying to start up a business making bodhráns! No-one had heard of such a thing. And trying to do it in Roundstone! Back in 1980 Connemara was very, very remote. We were down at the end of a lane at the end of Europe.'

Malachy picks up a wooden beater and rattles it across the taut skin of the round wooden drum – like a tambourine without the little cymbals – that he holds upright on his knee. He is beating out the rhythm of a jig, a simple 'one-two-three, one-two-three' that gradually takes on an astonishing complexity of tone and timbre as Malachy's fingers open and close, engage and disengage, scamper up and down the reverse side of the bodhrán's skin. 'That thing should be played with a sharp knife,' was the great piper Seamus Ennis's dismissive opinion of the

FAR LEFT Lough Corrib's smooth waters, just right for lazing with a fishing rod in hand.

ABOVE Malachy Bodhrán displays one of his peerless goatskin drums.

LEFT Putting the finishing touches to the work; a Celtic design is painted on to the skin.

goatskin drum whose beat accompanies Irish music. But in the hands of a master like Malachy, the bodhrán discovers an expressive voice of its own.

Malachy Bodhrán – real name Malachy Kearns – is not only a gifted player of the bodhrán; he is Ireland's acknowledged Master Maker of the drums, though the modest Malachy himself is uneasy with the title. 'The mantle doesn't fit,' he shrugs, 'I haven't enough grey hairs.' Roundstone bodhráns go out from Connemara to all corners of the world. When the leading singers and players of Irish traditional music are in need of a top-class bodhrán it is to the waterfront workshop of Malachy Bodhrán that they look. Many come in person to watch the fascinating process by which the drums are painstakingly brought into being.

Malachy picks his goatskins personally. Only the best will do, and not every goatskin will play true. 'The first Wednesday of every month,' he says, 'is the day when the goatskins are delivered, and the smell would knock you flat.' In an area of high unemployment, Roundstone Musical Instruments employs a handful of apprentices and skilled instrument makers in the workshop. The chosen skin has to be soaked and softened in water, then scraped clean. Then it is stretched, and fixed with glue and brass tacks to the frame of the bodhrán, a circle of beechwood or birch ply about 18 inches across. Bracing bars can be fitted inside the frame.

When the drum is ready, Malachy's wife Anne takes her turn in the process. She paints a Celtic design on the skin, using colourful dyes that soak into the very fibres of the goatskin and can stand up to the pounding of the wooden beater for decades on end without fading. 'I like to work in a Celtic style,' Anne says. 'It might be a harp, a bird or a dog, or perhaps a boat; or I might choose an elaborate capital letter. If I get the dye right, the design should last the owner's lifetime, anyway.'

Its wooden rim oiled and polished to a beautiful dull glow, the finished bodhrán might be packed up and sent anywhere in the world from Australia to Zanzibar. Or it might stay in the Roundstone workshop to be tested and bought – perhaps by a master musician for its superb sound qualities, perhaps by a passing tourist to hang as a feature decoration on the wall back home. 'Drum harder!' advises Malachy Bodhrán as he shakes a purchaser by the hand in cheerful farewell. 'Drum harder – live longer! Wallup!'

LEFT When Irish eyes are smiling… dreams of glory in a Gaelic Athletic Association shirt.

RIGHT The glorious crescent sweep of white shell sand in Dog's Bay, Co. Galway.

DISCHARGING THE CLOUD

The three ten-year-olds jostling towards me along the lane in back country Wexford might have been triplets. They were certainly blood relations, two sisters and their brother at a guess, all extravagantly freckled, red-haired and blue-eyed, all with that typical red-head's high blush in the cheeks. The late afternoon sun was angled right in their faces, lighting up enormous mocking grins as they shared some private joke. I caught the giggles as they scuffled past, a devil-may-care threesome, released from after-school detention, some wretched rural teacher's bane.

Just whose life they had been making a misery came clear as I rounded the bend. She was still leaning in the doorway of the primary school, her whole body slumped in an attitude of defeated exhaustion, eyes staring blankly in the wake of her tormentors. One hand scrabbled in her cardigan pocket and fished out an olive-green packet. 'Major' brand, I could tell at fifty paces: cheap and powerful. She stuck one in her mouth with a hand that shook like a cartoon hand, lit it without looking at it, and sucked in the smoke; then discharged the blue-grey cloud and let her shoulders sag against the door frame with a thunderous sigh, as if expelling the poison of the day from body and soul in one noxious gush.

HIGH OLD TIME

Ten o'clock on a drizzly morning in County Roscommon, driving through some prosaic little roadside village among wet fields under grey skies, mind in neutral, expecting nothing. Passing the primary school, eyes and brain suddenly snapped to attention. Out of the door came prancing a fabulous caravan of animals: a blue-faced bull, a lion, a beaked bird of prey, some kind of creature with a snake head. I pulled up, staring through the misted car window. A mouse with enormous ears, an Egyptian god-style dog, a giant blubber-mouthed fish, something black and spiky that I couldn't identify. Fantasy was confined to the upper half of each creature. From the waist down they were seven-year-old children in gym shorts and plimsolls, ecstatically capering through the school-yard puddles.

At the head of the procession cavorted a giant, twice the size of the animals, with an outsize pink papier-mâché face. It led the dance through the puddles, regardless of splashes, before turning back towards the school door. Inside the span of a minute the whole surrealistic cavalcade had disappeared once more. Lord alone knows what that inspired teacher and her class were celebrating or depicting. Whatever it was, they were having a high old time of it.

ROPE BRIDGE AT CARRICK-A-REDE

'Oh-my-God!' go the Antrim Coast tourists as they round the shoulder of cliff and look down on Carrick-a-Rede rope bridge. And it is a prime 'ooh-aah' sight, compelling and daunting in equal proportions. This is no ordinary footbridge, but a headspinning freak of human ingenuity. Swinging 80ft above the sea between a ledge in the cliff face and a craggy basalt island that rears offshore, the bridge is a cat's cradle of flimsy planks laid on

wires and braced with single hand-ropes. Watching a friend or relation totter in the middle of the 60-ft span as it bows under the weight and sways from side to side, loved ones safe on land look aghast, as if a joke has suddenly gone sour. Others take photographs or video sequences in malicious glee.

As soon as you go through the little entrance gate and step out onto the bridge, you sense that it is a living thing with a will of its own. It lurches sickeningly, the sideways swings increasing the further out you go. It slopes, alarmingly, to its low point halfway across. The plank decking seems unreasonably narrow. It jerks up and down to the rhythm of your steps. And the guide rope feels a sight too flimsy under your hands. Nevertheless, shrieking, giggling or cursing according to type, you get across and step with relief on to the top of Carrick-a-Rede. From here a path and steps snake down to an inlet where you find a little salmon fishery, the real raison d'être of the perilous rope bridge that has proved such a popular tourist attraction.

Wild Atlantic salmon swim along the Antrim coast, keeping close inshore. Carrick-a-Rede means 'Rock in the Road': the big basalt stack stands directly in the path of the fish, obliging them to turn aside. It may have been 350 years ago, perhaps more, that local fishermen realised how they could turn the obstacle to their own advantage by running a net out from the island to snare the diverted salmon. The ingenious rope bridge, fixed between mainland and Carrick-a-Rede each spring and taken down again in autumn at the end of the salmon season, gives the fishermen access to the fishery at the right time of year, and effectively safeguards the stocks at spawning time by its removal.

A simple construction, ecologically sound, environmentally friendly, as useful today as it was back in the seventeenth century, and no less frightening and exhilarating as a challenge to the nerves. Not that the locals see it that way. They stride nonchalantly across the bucking bridge with a casual sang-froid that the lily-livered tourist can only admire and envy.

'YOU CAN'T EAT SCENERY'

'I've thirty acres of a farm back there towards the Maumturks,' said the Connemara man, lying on his back by the roadside turf stack on Bóthar na Scrathóg and squinting up at the sun. 'Thirty acres of bog and grass and granite rock. There's no using any kind of farm machinery, not even a tractor or a plough, because of the rocks that are in it. You have to work this land with the spade, by hand. So there's not a living to be made from farming in these parts.

FAR LEFT Many people in rural Ireland are faced with a life of hard farming in a hard land.

LEFT Weatherbeaten, humorous, shaped by a lifetime's hard work – the face of an Irish countryman.

FOLLOWING PAGE The rocks and bogs of southern Connemara, with the Maumturk Mountains for a backdrop.

'How do I make a living? I go on the dole, mostly. I sell all the turf I can cut. Maybe sell some vegetables that we grow in our garden, though most of those we eat ourselves. I've a few sheep on the hill, and the government and the EU hand us down some subsidies. That's what keeps us going. There's no hope of anything better, so the young people are still leaving, trickling away to Galway city. This part of Connemara doesn't get the tourists like Clifden does, or out by Roundstone or up by Letterfrack. It's kind of betwixt and between. All the tourists want is for the landscape to stay as it is, beautiful and wild. But I think most of the people in Connemara would tell you they would rather see some factories built, even if it spoils the scenery. After all, it doesn't matter how beautiful the flowers are – you can't reach out and eat the flowers. You can't eat scenery.'

Chapter 4

LAST NIGHT'S FUN

'ARE YOU WORKING THE BAR AT ALL?
FIVE PINTS, MAN, AND MOVE IT!'

Dolores Keane at a session in the Small Bridge, Dingle, Co. Kerry

A slow soft afternoon, somewhere in County Mayo. A grey stone farmhouse

on a quiet bit of back road between three hills, not far from the sea. Patrick,

Mickey and I slosh through the puddles of the farmyard past a brand new

Japanese four-wheel-drive pickup, past the tumbledown ruins of an old

thatched cottage, and round the end of the modern stucco farmhouse that

stands alongside. Moisture freckles on the wind, more like the inside of a

cloud than anything as emphatic as rain.

The back door of the farmhouse opens and a tousle-haired man in rubber

boots looks out. 'Ah, lads,' is his terse greeting. The telephone call that Mickey

made an hour ago has forewarned him of our arrival. Wordlessly he leads us

round the bungalow and across the mucky cobbles to the old barn that

occupies one side of the farmyard. A flight of stone steps rises up the outside

LEFT Painted houses and pub signs add colour to a street in Sneem on the Ring of Kerry.

LEFT Plain living: cottage of a 'mountainy man' on the Dingle peninsula.

RIGHT 'At the foot of the hill there's a neat little still Where the smoke curls up to the sky...'

BELOW The innocent cottage doors of rural Ireland conceal many a secret.

of the barn. At the top of these the farmer unlocks a red-painted door and we troop inside. He shuts and locks the door carefully after us, then twitches a sack aside from the window over which it has been hanging; enough to let some daylight in on the scene.

In the whole bare length of this upper floor of the barn there is only one object – a heap of musty straw half covered with another mouldering sack. The farmer stoops and pulls back the sack, and we crane round to look down into a snug hollow in the straw where a dozen big glass flagons are dully winking in the soup-thick grey light. The farmer winks, too, as sly as a fox. He bends in to the straw heap and pulls out a flagon. The screw top spirals off with a little grating squeak. Out of the breast pocket of the farmer's jacket comes a tiny tumbler. He tips the flagon, and we all smell the scorching vegetable whiff as the tumbler fills.

The farmer holds up the glass to the window, checks the contents for clarity, then tosses the liquid well back into his throat. A couple of swallows and it is gone. I realise that this apparent host-first breach of manners is in fact a courtesy, albeit a practical one, demonstrating in the clearest possible way the distiller's faith in the non-toxic nature of his product. Reassured, the three of us take our turn – Mickey first, as the instigator of the transaction, then Patrick as the other known local face, and myself, the stranger, last. One by one we hold the little tumbler

up to the dim square of the barn window, sniff the liquid, and toss
it down. It hits the back of the mouth like a squirt of disinfectant,
and the throat closes momentarily against the jolt of pure alcohol.
Then the oily texture spreads round and across the inside of the
mouth, the opposing edges of the tongue seem to curl up towards
each other like a poppadom touching boiling oil, and a wash of
clean strong taste that is also a searing smell climbs up through
the nasal membranes into the brain cavity, where it spills forward
in tears to line the eye sockets.

'Ah,' says Patrick, watching me with a smile. 'The pure drop.'
The second glassful goes downwards into my stomach rather than
upwards into my head, and spreads a warm glow. Mickey nods
approval at the farmer, then pulls a flat wad of notes out of his
trouser pocket and hands over a few of them. He curls a
forefinger through the glass loops on the necks of two of the

flagons, and carries them one at each side out of the door and
down the flight of steps. Patrick and I follow; we have come along
as friends, for the ride and because we have each chipped in a few
pounds to the kitty, but Mickey, as the one who has set up the
sale and collected contributions from a dozen other sources, is the
one to carry the goods and take the risk of slipping in the
farmyard muck and seeing all that grade one poteen go, literally,
down the drain.

The farmer does not accompany us to our car, but ducks into
his back door after a lift of the hand and a gruff 'Good luck, then,
lads.' We put a rug over the two flagons and tuck a fold of it
between them to stop them banging into each other on the
potholed road from the farm. 'Good stuff,' pronounces Mickey, as
we drive off towards this evening's music session that now may
well turn into tomorrow's.

LEFT Ost na nOilean, the Hotel of the Isles, where the crack is mighty and all in Gaelic.

RIGHT Fishing provides a much-needed source of income in many impoverished rural communities.

THE RARE OLD MOUNTAIN DEW

Let breezes blow and the waters flow
In a free and easy way,
But give me enough of the rare old stuff
That's made near Galway Bay.
For policemen all from Donegal,
Sligo and Leitrim too,
We'll give them the slip and we'll take a little sip
Of the rare old mountain dew.

Hi the diddly-idle-dum, diddly-doodle-idle-dum
Diddly doo-ri-diddle-aye-day,
Hi the diddly-idle-dum, diddly-doodle-idle-dum
Diddly doo-ri-diddly-idle-day.

At the foot of the hill there's a neat little still
Where the smoke curls up to the sky;
By the smoke and the smell you can plainly tell
That there's poteen, boys, nearby.
For it fills the air with a perfume rare,
And betwixt both me and you,
As home we roll we could drink a bowl
Or a bucket of mountain dew.

Hi the diddly-idle-dum, diddly-doodle-idle-dum
Diddly doo-ri-diddle-aye-day,
Hi the diddly-idle-dum, diddly-doodle-idle-dum
Diddly doo-ri-diddly-idle-day.

NOT THE GAUGER

The red-headed young islander in the bar of Ost na nOilean approached me with great politeness, for he had a ticklish subject to broach. 'Excuse me,' he smiled, 'but would that have been you that I saw down on the beach on Furnace Island earlier today, looking across at Dinish? You had a notebook in your hand, I think. I saw you from my house.'

'Yes,' I said, 'that was me.' The young man looked surprised, and maybe reassured, to hear my English accent. But something was still making him uneasy. 'I wonder,' he said tentatively, 'if you would mind saying what it was you were writing in your book.'

'Oh, just some notes about the flowers and the shore birds,' I told him. 'A diary of a walk I'm doing.'

Relief spread across his freckled face like the sunrise. Later that evening the barman told me, confidentially, that they weren't really used to strangers on Furnace, nor here on Gorumna either, come to that, and they had all seen me wandering about scribbling in my notebook and had all been wondering about me. The red-haired young man – not too steady on his feet by this stage of the evening as he belted out a song in Gaelic – had spread the word that I might be the 'gauger', an official from the social security office. Many of the islanders were on the dole, said the barman, and supplementing that income by picking winkles along the shore and selling them on the black economy. Also, he murmured across the bar, Dinish had been a great place for poteen-making once upon a time, and not all the stills might be completely inactive even now. So I could see why a few questions might have needed to be asked.

This conversation took place in English, but most of the chatter and story-telling in Ost na nOilean, the Hotel of the Isles, was conducted in Gaelic that is still the first language of the little ragged-edged string of islands – Lettermore, Gorumna, Lettermullan, Furnace and Dinish – that curls into Galway Bay from the southern shore of Connemara. The ground is scabbed with granite, fields are tiny and rushy, the ground poor, the weather harsh. The inlets, choked with bright orange seaweed, lead to diminutive jetties used by a small handful of fishing boats. Life is tough here. But the islanders know how to enjoy themselves on a Saturday night out.

We had two songs from the red-haired winkle picker. A barrel-bellied man with a sweaty red bull's face, stomach swinging low out of the burst buttons on his shirt, skipped a delicate jig, his shoes with their dandy gold chains twinkling back and forth. A group of women dressed in their party best sat straight-backed at their table, six glasses of lemonade in front of them, and sang a beautiful slow lament in unison. Someone told jokes in Gaelic. The All-Ireland Under-15 Accordion Champion, another redhead,

ABOVE 'So anyway, up jumps yer man and he says to the other feller...' A story shared over a pint.

BELOW A melodeon player in a Westport pub, knocking a tune out of the old box.

borrowed the band-leader's melodeon and tore off a blindingly fast strip of reels, then sat eating a chocolate bar and blushing while people dropped him words of congratulation. By the end of the evening there were sixty or seventy people in the bar, roaring with conversation and music.

Everyone stood up, and almost everyone sang, when the band played the Irish national anthem to round things off at midnight. The doors were opened, and a haze of cigarette smoke rushed out ahead of the crowd. 'Good night to you, good night,' called the red-haired man, and he stumbled off down the road into a darkness lit by the phosphorescent glow and fade of surf.

THE DANCING STONE

You'd never find the Dancing Stone unless you knew where to look, in a thicket of hazels on a hillside not far from the townland of Letterbailey near the borders of Fermanagh and Tyrone. Up above Far Town you push your way in among the hazels. They grow so close, and whip your face and up-flung hands so smartly, that it seems as if they are trying to keep you away.

The Dancing Stone lies on the edge of a little dell, a big flat-topped slab the size of a table. The surface is pocked with rain holes and slick with moss and greasy leaf-drip from the overarching hazels. You have to be careful not to slip over, but if you walk out on to the Stone as if on to a dance floor and smack your heels down, you get a good solid ring.

The proximity of the hazel whips prevents you from trying any fancy stuff, but as you stand there you can imagine the Sundays of old when people from all over the district would make their way to the Dancing Stone. Men and women gave exhibitions on this natural platform for dancing, and clever-footed sets of four could cut a dash there, if rather a cramped one. In those days the hazels either did not grow on that hillside or were kept coppiced back, and there was a grand view out over the hills. You could use

ABOVE The Black Stuff: hard to pour, easy to drink, and the perfect companion to crack and music.

the Stone as a grandstand for singing too. And there were acres of good deep heather all around, just right for courting couples who wanted somewhere soft and springy to relax. So they will tell you down in Tempo, anyway.

'GOOD NIGHT TO YOU, GOOD NIGHT,'
CALLED THE RED-HAIRED MAN,
AND HE STUMBLED OFF DOWN THE ROAD.

BUTTER WOULDN'T MELT ...

'So anyway,' says Pat O'Hagan of Cookstown, the fruitiest
tall tale teller in County Tyrone, as I take the top off my first
pint of Guinness, 'thinks she to herself, the price of butter's
cheap on the south side of the border, and the price of butter's
dear on the north side of the border, so I'll take a couple of pound
of butter and I'll smuggle it from right to left, which is to say
from south to north.

'So she takes a great lump of butter and she puts it down
the front of her dress and wherever it is, and she sets off from

ABOVE Harsh granite outcrops
scab the bog of Gorumna Island,
Galway Bay.

RIGHT The traditional Irish pub: where
storytellers and musicians come to ply
their trade.

Carrickroe for Aughnacloy. But as she's crossing the border the
sergeant stops her and he says, very politely, "Will you please
come down to the barracks with me, ma'am?"

'Well, she has to go. 'Tis a cold night, and the barrack room
has a good fire going in the fireplace. "Sit down by the fire, ma'am,
won't you?" and she has to sit. The sergeant and a couple of men

sit with her, chatting away very pleasantly, and she can feel the butter beginning to run and trickle down under her dress and wherever it is.

'Of course, the sergeant and the constables know quite well what she's been up to. "Come on, lads," says the sergeant, "we'll nip out to the pub for a pint, and let this poor cold lady get herself warm." So out they go, laughing themselves into a black knot, and there she has to sit for an hour with the butter melting and staining the front of her dress and running down and out all across the barrack room floor.

'The policemen take their time, of course, but at last they come back in and find the woman soaked in butter from head to toe, and a gallon of melted butter all over the floor. The sergeant, he lets on not to notice. "Oh, ma'am, are you still here?" says he. "Of course you're free to go. We're glad to have our suspicions confounded," says he as the woman slithers and slides out the door all hot and bothered and as greasy as a bag of chips, "but, you see," says the sergeant, "we thought that you might be trying to smuggle butter. Goodnight, ma'am, goodnight."

LEFT On Clare Island in Clew Bay the pub opens around midnight. As for when it closes, well ...

BELOW Letting it go in a Mayo pub; a fiddler sunk in her own musical world.

RIGHT Into the pub for a little drop of medicine... Village pubs like this one at Ballyferriter on the Dingle peninsula are the social hubs of their communities.

DANCING AT KEADY

One o'clock in the morning in Stan Arthur's pub in Keady, County Armagh. It is a kind of a lock-in, in that no new customers have been admitted since last orders an hour and a half ago, and those who want to leave now have to be let individually out of the locked front door into the quiet rainy street.

In the back part of the bar two teenage girls have been ripping their way with flute and fiddle through a set of jigs. Sean has just finished singing his hysterical epic 'Transit Van', generating shouts of laughter. Now the teenagers strike up a reel, and there's a stir at the tables opposite as a group of eight youngsters rise to their feet. One girl kicks her high heels neatly under the table and takes her place in a foursome. The other four take station alongside. They jiggle their feet, partly to loosen them and partly as an expression of token embarrassment at being exposed in front of a crowd.

Then with an upward heave of the shoulders and a snap back of the head they are off, feet flicking in and out, shoes stamping, the girls' ponytails flying as they pass and repass, setting to partners, whirling round in a tightly-clasped basket of four, their reddening faces set in rictus smiles. The onlookers at the pub tables clap and stamp in time, and the occasional sharp 'hup!' of encouragement or whoop of approval goes up. The two teenage musicians never look up, even when one of the dancers loses his balance and crashes into the chairs. The fiddler is entirely absorbed in what her fingers are doing, while the flute-player has her eyes shut as if in a seventh heaven of blissful concentration.

The applause and table-thumping when the dance ends is loud enough to make the barman glance anxiously door-wards. A visit from the constabulary would not be the ideal way of rounding off the night ...

'MIGHTY SESSION!'

'Mighty Session!' shouts the poster in the window of the Small Bridge pub. 'Gerry O'Connor and friends! Tonight!'

In my ignorance I have never heard of Gerry O'Connor. But I am aware that the world and his music-loving girlfriend have come down to Dingle for the August holidays. The Small Bridge will be packed to the doors and beyond. So I get down there an hour before the session is due to begin and secure my place, a perch on the back of the bench seat where the musicians will sit to play. It's a good spot, high enough above the heads of the crowd to let me see all that goes on, in among the musicians so that I

can ease my G and D key harmonicas out of my pocket and play along if the mood is right and if I feel confident enough, far enough out of the limelight to be able to fade into the background as a spectator if the music takes off into some expert's heaven of complexity where I can't follow it. Whatever happens, I can sense already that the Small Bridge will be right at the heart of the crack in Dingle tonight.

The crack is a basically untranslatable commodity, but it has to do with fellow feeling, music, laughter, leg-pulling, drink, food, talk, jokes black or blithe, momentary madnesses, psychic electricity, barbaric glee and a thousand other sparks that fly in good company. It can be great crack to have your nephews and nieces to tea, or to reel drunkenly down the road at midnight with ten other tosspots, or to walk twenty miles around the Mountains of Mourne with one good friend, or to roar out obscenely witty songs at a football match. Or, as in the case of the Small Bridge and its Mighty Session, to lay into a dozen tunes you have never heard before in the company of players so carelessly accomplished that they carry you along like a magic carpet, so far above your customary level of musicianship that next morning you will still be gasping from the rarefied air of the session and asking yourself if everything really did happen as your memory insists it did.

By ten o'clock this night the Small Bridge is literally heaving with people. How does Muiris Ferris behind the bar keep his cool, with a dozen customers clamouring for precedence at any one moment and twenty requests and countermanded orders hanging in the air? There could well be three hundred people crammed into this smallish pub. Those outside are standing on tiptoe on the windowsills, their disembodied heads inserted into the room like waxwork decapitees. German, Swedish, French, English,

American, Australian, Irish, Swiss, Danish, Italian and Scots accents war in mid-air. Sweat, makeup and drink run in torrents. The heat is all but unbearable.

Gerry O'Connor, an amiable young man with a neck-hugging mane of black hair, turns out to be one of Ireland's best-known traditional musicians. His fiddle playing is breathtaking. When he lays down the fiddle and picks up his banjo, everyone sighs in anticipation. Soon I see why. Gerry's fingers fly like birds off a wire. The plain plinky-plunky timbre of the banjo becomes expressive, dynamic. This is music as she should be played. The crowd parts as if shoved from the rear by a bulldozer.

A generously constructed woman with a waterfall of auburn hair down her back elbows her way through, a flute-case in each hand. The mandolin player and the beater of the bodhrán budge up, and she subsides between them. This is Dolores Keane, one of the most famous names in Irish traditional music, an earthquake of a woman. Soon Dolores will produce flute music to have the listeners jigging where they stand, jammed. She will sing, hoarsely but beautifully. Just now, though, Dolores is climbing to her feet again in an eruption of indignation, having spotted that every glass on the musicians' table is empty. 'Muiris!' she roars, cutting across the babble in the Small Bridge. 'Are you working the bar at all? Five pints, man, and move it!'

'MIGHTY SESSION!' SHOUTS THE POSTER IN THE WINDOW OF THE SMALL BRIDGE PUB. 'GERRY O'CONNOR AND FRIENDS! TONIGHT!'

CEILIDH HOUSE

Owen Smith's ceilidh house stands out at Fernagh, in the green
and purple boglands to the east of Omagh. It is a low-built place,
a traditional-looking house in a yard cobbled with tiny pebbles set
on end, with a byre and other off-buildings near at hand. But this
cottage is far neater and cleaner than you would expect any
working farmhouse to be. Owen Smith has restored it himself,
painstakingly, with the aim of reviving in County Tyrone a long-
dormant custom, the pleasant and neighbourly tradition of the
ceilidh. During thirty years of the Troubles, people were reluctant
to venture out to a lonely farm late at night. But in these easier
days the ceilidh seems like a great idea, a bit of fun and bonding
with friends and strangers.

A ceilidh can incorporate a dance, though you do not need to
have a dance in order to have a ceilidh. A ceilidh is simply a social
gathering. Anyone can attend, and everyone is welcome to
contribute something to the success of the ceilidh in a song, a
tune, a story, a trick or a bit of dancing. Tonight fifty people are
packed into the lamp-lit kitchen, forming loose concentric rings
round the local musicians, story-tellers and poets who sit at the
nucleus of this gathering. Some of these performers are celebrated
internationally; they have trodden the boards of famous venues
across the world from Carnegie Hall to Carnival in Rio. Others will
never gain a flicker of recognition beyond their home villages of
Carrickmore, Sixmilecross or Greencastle.

ABOVE Owen Smith's ceilidh
house out in the Tyrone bogland,
a gathering place for musicians.

RIGHT The session is warming up ...
crack at the ceilidh in
Owen Smith's.

Tonight the stars of the ceilidh are a ten-year-old girl who plays the whistle with the abandon of a blackbird, and the octogenarian fiddler who accompanies her with a technique as scurrying and spectacular as if the Devil were at his heels. But ceilidh is not really about star performances. With someone's breath down your neck and someone else's jacketed back pressed into your knees, you find your critical faculties drifting loose and wide. That tiny girl and her great-grandfatherly accompanist may be wonderfully talented. But it is the ensemble effect of fifty untrained voices singing 'The Parting Glass' that brings tears to your eyes at one in the morning, and the neatness of the local doggerel-belter's teasing of his neighbours that seems like the funniest thing you have ever heard an hour afterwards.

This ceilidh does not run on alcohol. A cup of tea and a sandwich around midnight is what keeps most people going, though a couple of ceilidh-makers have brought six-packs of beer with them. By two o'clock in the morning the songs are beginning to dry up and the octogenarian fiddle player has gone home, though younger hands have taken over and look as if they intend to keep it up all night.

The last of them reels off around dawn. Owen Smith throws a couple of sweet papers into the turf embers, looks around the quiet parlour and locks up. There's a big smile on his face as he drives back towards Omagh across the empty boglands with the sun behind him.

THE DRUNKEN FIDDLER

Inscription on a fiddle-shaped memorial stone by the ruined lodge at the entrance to Castle Caldwell, County Fermanagh:

'To Denis McCabe, Fidler, who fell out of the St Patrick barge belonging to Sir James Caldwell, Bart and Count of Milan, and was drown'd off the point. August ye 13th 1770.

BELOW Rural Ireland harbours many
fine musicians; here, a fiddler helps
the tune along at a session.

Beware ye fidlers of ye fidlers fate,

Nor tempt ye deep least ye repent to late;

Ye ever have been deemed to water foes -

Then shun ye lake till it with whiskey floes.

On firm land only exercise your skill;

There you may play and drink your fill.'

EEL-OIL

'So anyway,' Pat O'Hagan says, while the creamy bubbles swirl through my third pint of Guinness as it stands half-poured on the wooden casing that covers the stout taps, 'she gets your man up to the altar and back to the house where she slams the door behind them, and that's the last that any of us sees of them for a while. But not the last that anyone hears of them. Every time you'd walk past the house, there'd be this mighty roaring as the bride gave out to her beloved:

' "No! you're not going out to the pub tonight."

' "No! you're not smoking that dirty ould pipe."

' "No! you're not letting your bristles grow all week."

'Anyway, after a month or so we're in the pub one night and we hear this kind of groaning or lamentation coming from the back room. Ee-oi, ee-oi, it goes like a donkey. So we go round and we find your man himself, the reluctant bridegroom. He's sprawled out all over the table, dead drunk amid a heap of bottles, with his pipe blazing in his mouth and a week's whiskers on his chin, and he's groaning, "Eel-oil, eel-oil, eel-oil."

' "Paddy," we ask him, "what the devil ails you?"

' "Oh God, boys, eel-oil," says he. "I could put up with her roaring, and I could put up with her ban on me drinking, and I could put up with her ban on me ould pipe, and I could just about put up with her ban on me bristles. But when I saw her stripped for action at bedtime," says Paddy, "and when I saw her rub herself all over with eel-oil like her mama told her to do, that's when I realised that the marriage mightn't be a great success." '

It's a two-minute story: just long enough to allow the Guinness on the bar to settle and darken to the velvety black of the properly drinkable pint.

BRIGHT EYES AND GOOD INTENTIONS

A winter's night in Doolin, down on the coast of north-west Clare. A stag party from Dublin has braved the November wind and rain and crossed the country to take over O'Connor's famous music pub for the night. They are packed inside, forty strong, roaring out 'I remember Dublin in the rare old times'. Up the lane at McGann's, though, the wooden-walled bar is all but empty. The bad weather has detained most of the locals at home this evening, and the tourists that kept Teresa McGann's till ringing all summer departed with the swallows two months ago. There will be no more mighty sessions in McGann's, with bodhrán players from Switzerland and fiddlers from Australia, guitarists down from Norway and melodeon players up from South Africa, until next spring.

LEFT AND ABOVE 'A pint of porter is your only man' (Myles na gCopaleen). By some magic, Guinness tastes better in Ireland than anywhere else.

RIGHT 'Hush for the singer, now...' The song and the pint – what the ballad session is all about.

But there is still a ghost of music in the bar, where two players sit on hard chairs in front of the fire, absorbed in a tune. On the left is a bullet-headed guitar player, his shoulders hunched over his instrument, his right foot lifting with the upbeat and slapping quietly down on the floor with the downbeat. On the right a thin young man plays concertina, also hunched forward into the music. The skin on the backs of his hands bunches and smoothes as the straps tighten and loosen to the rhythm of his fingers, which are picking out the wobbles and stutters of embellishment that go with the tune they are playing around with: 'The End Of The Day'. In a crowded session on a summer's night in McGann's they might run 'The End Of The Day' three or four times through before switching to another tune, but here on this night there are no other players, no audience, no concessions to be made at all. So they doodle through 'The End Of The Day' for the umpteenth time, the guitarist hammering off and hammering on and trying little bass runs that sound more like jazz or salsa than an accompaniment to a traditional Irish tune, the concertina player wobbling and stuttering, squeezing some notes shut and opening others into the spaces between the places where the dots would go if this tune was written down. They are far away, together but separate, playing with and around each other but also for themselves. To a casual listener the music sounds thin, at times tentative, its richness unfolding only slowly and as part of the whole ambience of the room, the smell of the guitar player's cigarette smouldering forgotten in the ashtray, the soft tap of rain on the window, the red glow of the fire.

The door opens and three late-middle-aged Americans, a man and two women, blow in, shaking the rain from their Burberrys. They order three hot whiskeys, and then become aware of the musicians at the far end of the room. One of the women raises a

'WHEN I SAW HER RUB HERSELF ALL OVER WITH EEL-OIL I REALISED THE MARRIAGE MIGHTN'T BE A GREAT SUCCESS.'

finger to her lips, an exaggerated gesture that draws the stares of the two or three locals in the bar. The Americans tiptoe over with their hot whiskeys and settle at a table near the musicians, casting each other gleefully conspiratorial glances. They told us at the hotel we could hear wonderful Irish jigs in Doolin, and here they are! The three incomers lean forward in their rustling raincoats, impatient for the tune to end so that their applause may set the seal of an audience's appreciation on what they clearly see as a performance.

There is a change in the players' body language, a flicker of connecting glances between the two of them as they come down from the place they have played themselves up to. It is no surprise when they wind up 'The End Of The Day' in short order. The quiet patter of the Americans' hands, the little chirrups of pleasure, words of congratulation and polite request to hear 'Molly Malone' cause the two musicians to rise. The mumbled excuses sound a little churlish, but they are not

meant that way. The guitar player picks up his packet of cigarettes and they stroll off to the bar. The three Americans look at each other, puzzled, a little hurt. What happened there? Was it something we said?

It is tough luck on them. Tough luck that they did not drive a few hundred yards further along the lane to O'Connor's, where their applause and requests would have been just the ticket. Tough luck that they happened first on McGann's, and blundered in on a spell of magic too flimsy to withstand their bright eyes and good intentions.

HOT SPOON

'Well,' says Johny McKeagney, lowering his voice conspiratorially to draw my ear a little closer to his story, 'I'll tell you what they used to do back in the old days for a bit of fun, before television or the radio or any of that, when everyone had to make their own entertainment, even if it was rough humour, a lot of it.

'What we would do is, we would get a teaspoon and we'd push the handle of it into the fire and let it get scorching hot, and then we'd offer the spoon to the person we were playing the trick on, very politely, handle first, so that they'd sting their fingers when they took hold of it.

'Well, this particular clever boy thought he'd see could he trick the priest like that when he next called in at the house for a cup of tea. That would have been very daring in those days, to try and sting the fingers of a priest with the old hot spoon trick. But anyway, this priest mustn't have been as green as he was cabbage-looking, or maybe he'd played the same trick himself when he was a young one, because when the boy passed him the cup of tea with the hot spoon in the saucer he passed it on to the man of the house who was sitting alongside him!

'This lad is absolutely horrified, and he dives in with some excuse and grabs the saucer before his father can pick up the hot

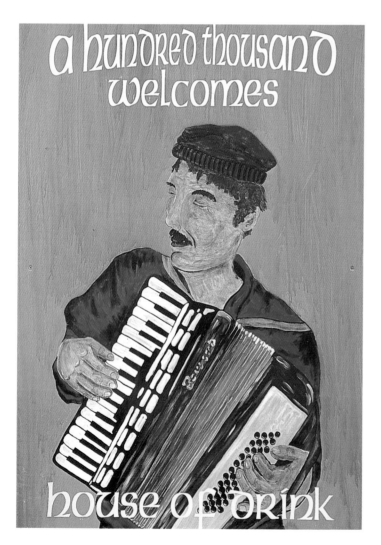

a hundred thousand welcomes

house of drink

LEFT House of drink … and house of music, too, at Louisburgh on Clew Bay, Co. Mayo.

RIGHT All smiles from the listeners, all concentration from the players as the tune takes off.

spoon. And then of course he has to pick up the spoon himself and stir the tea with it as if nothing's happening, with the tears of pain running out of his eyes and the red-hot handle blistering his fingers, and the eyes of this sly old priest winking at him over the teacup ...!'

JUMPING ON THE TRAIN

McGovern's pub in the little Fermanagh village of Derrygonnelly, round about midnight. In the back bar an 18th birthday party is at maximum roar, the disco so loud that its shock waves cause ripples on the surface of the lagoon of spilt beer on the bar top. In

TO A CASUAL LISTENER THE MUSIC SOUNDS THIN, AT TIMES TENTATIVE, ITS RICHNESS UNFOLDING ONLY SLOWLY AND AS PART OF THE WHOLE AMBIENCE OF THE ROOM.

the front bar, a session of traditional music is at full tilt. A row of players sits along benches and chairs, forced into an unnatural and unsessionlike straight line formation by sheer pressure of people in the bar. The box-player looks as if he is about to burst into flames from internal combustion. The guitar player has tried playing while sitting down, but keeps having the neck of her instrument jolted by drinkers shoving their way to and from the bar. So now she has adopted a curious stance, a kind of high crouch up on one of the chairs, which gets her chord hand above the crowd.

Jim Hoy, whom I have met for the first time earlier in the day, has his fiddle under his chin and cannot speak and play at the same time, but as I come into his field of vision he rolls his eyes in a gesture of recognition and jerks his head, inviting me to sit on a squeeze-box case, the only unoccupied flat surface in the room. The noise is unbelievable, a combination of the natural backwash of till jangle, glass clash and bark of shouted conversation, the heavy rhythmic thud of drum'n'bass that pulses through from the back bar birthday party along with shouts, cries and hoarse, drunken laughter, and the row that the players are kicking up as they tear at breakneck speed through 'Banish Misfortune'.

This is neither the time nor the place for fine delicate musical noodlings. The session and the disco have mingled and cross-fertilized. They are not steering in the same musical direction: far from it. 'Banish Misfortune' scurries in and out of the bass thud, sometimes part of it, sometimes slashing across it anti-rhythmically, anyway in another key (if drum'n'bass has a key). But the players have caught the simple energy of the party's soundtrack and are scrubbing away at their instruments at a hundred miles an hour. Maybe they are just trying to make themselves heard above the din by creating even more din.

It is a discordant, smeary, approximate way to play, and purists would no doubt be horrified. But if there are any purists in McGovern's tonight, their profile is low. There are problems in getting involved in a session like this – if I pull my harmonica out of my pocket and hop aboard the 'Banish Misfortune' train the next time she comes around, I will get sucked in and will not disengage myself until long past the time when any rural taxi driver would want to pick me up and take me to my night's lodging a dozen miles off on the shore of Lough Erne.

But I jump on, anyway.

RIGHT 'A quiet word, now!' Three's a crowd in a pavement conversation in small-town Ireland.

LEFT 'There was a dozen Swedish bodhrán players in the bar, so your man takes his fiddle out and gives the tune to the street...'

Chapter 5
AROUND THE WORLD FOR SPORT

'LAST ONE OUT, PULL THE DOOR TO!'

Leader of the Armagh Rhymers at Hallowe'en on Navan Hill Fort

'Please help me, I'm falling,

But that would be sin;

Close the door to temptation,

Don't let me walk in.'

LEFT The runners and riders at Ballybunion Races, Co. Clare. Horse racing is an eagerly followed sport in Ireland.

The words of the corny old song float out across the ballroom on a schmaltzy sea of vibrato-rich organ chords. Temptation and sin look about the last thing on the minds of the hundred couples who are one-two-three, one-two-threeing up and down. A public dance on a chilly autumn morning in the respectable spa town of Lisdoonvarna is not exactly the time and place to get down and get jiggy with your partner, even given such an opportunity as the annual ritual of the town's Matchmaking Festival.

The 60-year-old man with the brand new orange shoes and the sulphur-yellow poloneck sweater is doing well, though sweating heavily with exertion or nerves, as he steers a substantial lady in a floral poncho past the organist. Neither waltzer is looking into the face of the other: their eyes are fixed decorously in the middle distance beyond their partner's back. The same polite reserve can be seen in the expressions of most dancers in this 'ballroom of romance', whether light and easy on their feet or left-footedly clumsy. This noon dance, far from being a pick-up venue, is a vehicle for middle-aged singletons – spinsters or bachelors, widowed or parted – to let themselves gently into the festival mood, cushioned by plenty of ritual and formality.

Many of the festival-goers are lonely people left high and dry on tiny farms, fourth or fifth sons and daughters of the large families so common fifty years ago in devoutly Roman Catholic rural Ireland, too poor and by now too unattractive a prospect to find a marriage partner easily, of the wrong generation and moral persuasion to enjoy a sexually carefree late middle age. Most have come down for the matchmaking with no real intention of making a match; they are here with brothers, sisters or cousins to have a bit of a step-out and a few days of fun, with

ABOVE Lisdoonvarna matchmaking: 'Why don't you have a word with the tangler?'

RIGHT Taking it slow and steady: a quiet afternoon drink in Kenmare, Co. Kerry.

entertainment laid on throughout the festival. There will be the noon dances, like this one at the spa wells that first made Lisdoonvarna's prosperity back in the eighteenth century. There will be a ceremonial taking of the hydrogen sulphide-flavoured waters, a stroll or two, tea-dances out at Ballinalacken Castle, and a dozen evening dances to choose from in and around the town. Singles may indeed meet the partner of their dreams; but the matchmaking festival is generally where things get started, rather than consummated. Take it easy, is the Lisdoonvarna watchword. It's surprising how many dancing partners hook up a year or so later, somewhere else: 'Oh, didn't I meet you up at Lisdoonvarna? Well now, this is nice. And what are you doing this evening ...?'

It was the rise of Lisdoonvarna as a fashionable spa that ushered in the matchmaking. The kind of well-to-do farmers and rural men of business who patronised the place a couple of hundred years ago had dealing and bartering in their blood. What could be more natural than to bring those hard-to-place sons and daughters down to County Clare's premier resort for a few weeks, and fix them up with the best deal by way of a partner that the 'tangler' could broker? Tanglers were essentially middlemen who made a living by bringing buyers and sellers together across the whole spectrum of the rural economy – animals, land, property and so on. At Lisdoonvarna, armed with information about his clients, the tangler would put his canniness and nose for a deal to work in forging introductions between young people who might suit each other, and more importantly each other's parents. The Lisdoonvarna matchmaking lasted as a serious proposition until cheap package holidays abroad and an increasing disregard by young people for social conventions all but put an end to it in the 1960s. Nowadays it is in vigorous revival, partly a tourist enterprise, partly a media circus, partly what it has always been – a way of bringing shy and lonely country people together.

'I wonder will you be out at Ballinalacken this afternoon?' the polo-neck man asks his poncho'd partner, with a diffidence that belies his bright attire, as he walks her off the dance floor to her seat. 'Well, I may be,' she says, 'if I can find a lift,' and she gives him something not too far short of an encouraging smile.

GOOD LUCK FR CASEY'S

Eight o'clock on a Monday morning in early September, and not a dog stirs in the streets of Abbeyfeale. My footfalls as I limp out of town are the loudest sound around. I am walking gingerly, wincing at every stumble – not because of blisters or other road damage, but due to the presence of a bodhrán drummer crashing around unmercifully in the dusty boxroom of my brain. Judging by the deathly, whey-faced stillness that hangs over Abbeyfeale this morning, he is in occupation of most heads in the little West Limerick market town.

From a plinth in the town square, Father William Casey faces up the street. Something strange has happened to him overnight. He seems to be making a Black Power salute, his upraised right hand clad in a shiny black leather gauntlet. Closer inspection reveals the exotic handwear to be masking tape, from which dangles a home-made flag striped in blue and white. The football jersey knotted by its sleeves round Father Casey's shoulders is in blue and white stripes, too. So is the lettering on the banner

draped from house to house across the street, at which the statue of the priest stares with empty eyes. 'Good Luck Fr Casey's' reads the banner.

Father Casey won his place in the hearts of Abbeyfeale people by his support of their struggle for land reform in the 1870s. That place has been reconsolidated this morning through the triumph of the town's Gaelic football team that bears his name. Yesterday evening, flushed with a three-goal victory in the cup final over their rivals the Galtee Gaels, Father Casey's team brought the County Limerick Gaelic football championship trophy home to Abbeyfeale. The townsfolk turned out to line the streets, waving everything blue and white from home-crafted flags to plastic bags from the supermarket. The team captain was borne into town on the bonnet of a car, brandishing the cup like a war trophy to left and right as the children screamed deliriously from the pavements. The team followed, swaying on the open trailer of a lorry with their arms round each other's shoulders in a tight, masculine huddle, every man roaring, 'Olé-olé-olé-olé!' Behind

LEFT Nice and easy does it: taking a rest on a peaceful afternoon in small-town Donegal.

RIGHT Colourful painted houses and pubs in the aptly-named Rainbow Street in Kiltamagh, Co. Mayo.

them the half of the town that was not going bananas on the sidewalks was packed into cars and crocodiling up the street, with horns blaring and boisterous youths halfway out of the rolled-down windows beating out olé-olé-olé-olé in rhythm on the car roofs. It was a mighty noise and spectacle, followed by an almighty communal night on the town.

Propped against Father Casey's plinth and trying to nerve myself for a hangover morning's footslogging into the Glanaruddery Mountains, I glance over the inscription under the flag-dangling statue. 'He found his people struggling in the toils

of landlordism,' it reads. 'He left them owners of the soil and freemen.' The great-great-grandsons of those freemen kept it up in the pub until three o'clock this morning, when a large policeman entered – brave man – to enforce the law relating to licensing hours. He must have been the only man in Abbeyfeale not to have drink taken. The roar that greeted his stolid request for the personal details of all present was almost as loud as that raised for Father Casey's team a few hours before. Blearily, I now seem to remember trying not to giggle as he solemnly noted my name and address: Winston Spencer Churchill, Toffington

Towers, Snob Street, London. What I cannot recall is any appearance of a policemanly tongue in cheek. Perhaps he was a Galtee Gaels fan.

Groaning to myself, limping and wincing, I slouch on out of town, a sadder but sadly not a wiser man. Father Casey watches me go, the vestige of a smile on his green bronze lips.

HALLOWE'EN AT NAVAN

A mild October night, and the cloudy sky over Armagh pops and crackles. A rocket shoots up from one of the city's housing estates and bursts in a dandelion-head of green and blue, its sparks showering down towards St Patrick's Roman Catholic Cathedral. Along the horizon is a flicker of orange light from bonfires in back gardens and on waste ground, and a blink-blink of blue emergency lamps. Hallowe'en is a busy time for Irish firemen.

Tonight is All Souls' Night, when every self-respecting ghoulie, ghostie and long-leggit beastie is out on the town. Children in witch masks and black cloaks flutter about the streets, swinging pumpkin lanterns. Their ancestors' childhood revels would have been lit with lamps made of hollowed-out turnips, paraded around the 'bonefires'. The English tidied up the wilder strands of this midwinter fire ceremony under the banner of Guy Fawkes, but here in Armagh it comes full strength as an echo from a pagan past.

No better place to be at Hallowe'en than Navan, the great Iron Age hill fort that overlooks Armagh from the western side of the city. An air of mystery and dark magic clings to the green mound – Eamhain Mhachan or Queen Macha's Palace, to give the monument its ancient Irish name – along with a rich stew of potent legends from Ireland's mythical past.

Three strange figures pace the arena of the circular, turf-roofed Navan Centre. Basketwork hoods cover their faces, cornstalks sprout from their heads and waists. Rags and ribbons flutter from their limbs. They are the Armagh Rhymers, Lords of Misrule this Hallowe'en night; part mummers, part Morris men, part gods of fertility and green magic.

They shuffle and sway, banging on skin drums, chanting snatches of poetry and songs – some rooted in the folklore of Armagh, others harvested from the furthest corners of Ireland – to evoke the madness and mystery of Hallowe'en. We form in line behind the three faceless ones, and they lead us out, still singing and reciting, into the night. A bonfire blazes nearby, and here

long torches are pushed into the flames. By streaming torchlight we process under the trees and along pathways, through a gate and up the slippery grass side of the hill fort to cross its great ditches. Then up again, climbing the last steep slope to the flat-topped dome at its summit where a night-time panorama of lights twinkles across the dark Armagh countryside around the distant, floodlit shapes of the city's two cathedrals on their opposing hills.

There would be magic enough on any hilltop in the dead of night, especially one lit by fire from smoking torches. But this smooth-turfed summit holds its own remarkable secrets, whispers of pre-Christian rituals whose nature can still only be guessed at, in spite of all that excavating archaeologists have been able to discover. Under our feet, as we gather in a circle around the three masked Rhymers, lies a gigantic mound of stones, more than a hundred feet from side to side. The stones were piled up inside an enormous wooden building on the heights of Navan by Iron Age tribesmen in 94 BC – tree-ring dating of the remaining timber posts has fixed the date precisely. After all that planning, organisation and labour, the constructors then set fire to the building, deliberately burning it down over its huge mound of stones. Then they turfed it over. What goddess or fierce facet of nature they were worshipping or placating, no-one knows for sure.

Present-day worshippers of arcane forces have got here before us tonight. We come up over the lip of the mound behind the Rhymers to find two figures seated cross-legged in the centre of the summit, floppy black hats on their heads, a fire of turf blocks flickering in a brick hearth at their feet. A ring of rope encircles them, perhaps to keep out the Prince of Darkness and his cohorts.

What they make of the crowd of cheerful singers and hand-clappers that have suddenly broken in on their activities, we never find out. The two arcanists continue to sit silently in our midst, faces lowered to their fire, staring into their own private universe. The man standing next to me is not impressed. 'There's wiser ones eating grass,' he mutters; a judgement that sends his neighbours into giggles.

RIGHT Cat and dog maintain a
sleepy truce in Roundstone,
Connemara.

The Armagh Rhymers intone a burst of poetry, produce guitars and a concertina and lead us in a round of singalong songs. 'The boys won't leave the girls alone,' chant the revellers, clapping time. These are songs of childhood, jingles that everyone knows – even the two silent squatters on the hilltop, judging by the rhythmic in-spite-of-themselves tapping of their feet. 'Last one out, pull the door to!' cries the Rhymers' leader, and we slowly descend the slopes and leave the mound to its cabalistic occupants.

LOUGH LAZING

The Joyce River gushes out of the flank of Leenaun Hill and tumbles into the Maam Valley, where it veers south-east to snake down to Lough Corrib. The beautiful deep-water inlet of Killary Harbour, cradled in the curved arms of mountains, lies only two miles north-west of where the river springs from the hill. If it were not for these two miles of steep valley, Connemara would be an island.

County Galway's ragged-edged western outpost is defined by its salt water margin, the famous sea-bitten coast that has attracted admirers ever since the Romantics taught us the allure of rose-tinted spectacles. And the heart of this all-but-island, too, is full of water – bog pools, streamlets, backwaters and hundreds of loughs or lakes.

Lough Corrib is the mightiest of these, a great dolphin-shaped sheet of water 25 miles long that outlines the whole of the far eastern flank of Connemara. When you laze back in a rowing boat in the centre of Lough Corrib on a misty still afternoon, your fishing rod idle in your hands, the distant mountains milky with rain that is bypassing the lake, you can feel yourself as near to heaven as poor sinners are allowed to come, even in Ireland. The clinker-built wooden shell rocks slightly as the oarsman shifts on his thwart and feels for a cigarette, but there is a heavy oiliness or silkiness to the water that causes the ripples to flatten to a matt sheen a few yards out from the boat. The scrape of the match and 'pop' of the smoker's lips as he inhales are the only sounds. Three floats sit upright, their black nether sections concealed in

LEFT A little skiff and a long
afternoon: boating on Lough
Corrib, Co. Galway.

the lake, their orange upper halves jutting clear like the shoulders of miniature swimmers treading water. With a motion so smooth and quiet that no-one even notices for a second or two, one of the floats slips under. The quick tug that follows is not on your line; so you can look on serenely, stunned under the dreamy spell of the afternoon, even while the spike-backed lake perch is brought inboard in a blurry wriggle of green and silver. The energy of the other fishermen, their enthusiasm over the catch, seem part of some parallel world of action. There is a film of unreality between you and them. But to whisk you back through the gauze would only take a twitch of your rod tip, the jerk of communication between your hands and a gristle-lipped mouth that may even at this moment be shaping to close on your hook.

KEEPIE-UPPIE

The young boy playing keepie-uppie by the gate of the Gaelic Athletic Association ground on the outskirts of Crossmolina looks about eight years old. He is playing a game of virtual hurling in his private skull stadium, and brandishing what must be his older brother's new hurley as he does so. He himself is hardly longer

ABOVE It takes a subtle eye and a practised hand to shape a hurley properly.

LEFT Hurling with the best of them: young players at a game in Tralee, Co. Kerry.

RIGHT 'Now, then, you lovely ladies, get 'em down quick!' Bookies chalk the odds at Ballybunion Races.

than the thick wooden stick with the curved end. Instead of a ball he is using a chunk of rock that rebounds from the blade of the hurley every second with the 'thunk' of indenting wood. If the brother could see him now, he'd kill him. He'll kill him tonight, anyway, when he finds out what the little so-and-so has done to his prized hurley.

What this lad is doing hanging around the GAA ground is anybody's guess. It is the middle of a weekday morning, and he ought to be in school. What he is day-dreaming of, absent-mindedly bouncing the rock off the hurley and grinning in through the gate at the empty stands and the deserted pitch, is easier to imagine.

DINGLE SHOW

Aloysius danced alone, and not happily. His blue-speckled teeshirt and grubby green tracksuit trousers made him self-conscious among the other seven-year-old entrants for the Irish dancing competition at Dingle Show. All the other boys had been kitted out by their mothers in neat white shirts and dark school trousers, all the girls in beautifully embroidered black velvet dresses with lace collars and full short skirts. And it wasn't easy to remember the sequence of the steps, all on his own up on the back of the lorry where everyone at the show seemed to be staring at him, with the girls off at one side giggling behind their hands, the melodeon player going too fast, and his teacher glowering as she loomed nearby and hissed out of the corner of her mouth, 'Come on, now, Aloysius, don't forget everything you've learned.' It was a relief, both to Aloysius and to the onlookers, when the accompanist cut the dance short and allowed him to walk off, stiff-legged with mortification.

Down at the bottom of the sloping concrete apron of Dingle beast mart, horses tossed their heads nervously as handlers led them round and round a stone-walled pound. Men leaned on the wall to watch the horses, while their young sons perched beside them. Men and boys had identical cloth caps on backs of heads, grass blades in mouths and set seriousness of expression. No frivolity down here among the heavy basic scents of dung, straw, tobacco and the sweet smell of horses. It was a man thing. The

LEFT Only the very best will do as
young Irish dancers compete at the
Fleadh Nua in Ennis, Co. Clare.

RIGHT Spinning by wheel
and sleight of wrist, the old-
fashioned way.

girl thing was taking place up in the market buildings: the
judging of fruit cakes by the women, and the costuming of dogs
by their daughters for the title of Best Dressed Dog in Dingle.
More miserable even than Aloysius, the dogs cowered in
celluloid collars and bowler hats, heads lowered in shame, tails
between legs. One girl had managed to force the family's Jack
Russell into a doll's pink cardigan, which he was occupied in
removing shred by shred while his young mistress howled her
eyes out.

On a piece of level ground behind the mart buildings, men
were bowling for a pig. A couple of drunks went reeling over a
straw bale and collapsed in a heap, too far gone to fight. Up on the
back of the lorry, little girls with numbers pinned to their bodices
were dancing in pairs to the jerky driving sound of the melodeon.
Pink knees bent and straightened, white-stockinged legs flickered
in front of and behind each other, and curls and ponytails
bounced up and down as they danced with ramrod backs and

hands held stiffly by their sides, skirts billowing up and subsiding,
faces expressionless – little experts. Number One, a pretty and
self-aware six-year-old, had scabbed her knees just before Dingle
Show, but was clearly going to scoop the pool of prizes despite not
looking her best.

A stone's throw away, the souvenir shops and cafés of Dingle
were jam-packed with tourists. Here at the Show it was almost
all locals, many speaking Irish, all intent on the business of
buying, selling and winning prizes. Number One skipped off
with her arms full of chrome-twinkling trophies for the living
room cabinet. A mongrel in a poke bonnet won Best Dressed
Dog in Dingle. Aloysius restored his self-respect with an outsize
triple-cone ice cream. Only the dancing teacher was still
looking grim at going-home time, but maybe that was just the
natural look of the poor creature, as I overheard one parent
murmur to another.

LEFT 'Me mam made it – took her for
ever...!' A sample of beautiful hand-
sewn embroidery.

Chapter 6

THE IVY ON THE WALL

'LITTLE MONUMENTS, YOU KNOW –
MONUMENTS TO ALL THAT SUFFERING.'

Maryangela Keane on a Famine Road in the Burren, Co. Clare

Leaning on the wind and looking over the cliffs of Inishmore, I gasped in

fear and delight to see a great wave rise at me from the depths 300 feet

below. It climbed steadily up the sheer black wall of the cliff, milky-blue

with air bubbles, its hissing swelling to a roar, until a lip of foam curled back

and over and it bowed down and away, melting into the next oncoming surge.

These right-angle cliffs of Aran, mighty and dark, face the sea as if they

would continue to break up its attack for ever. But you only have to spend

a mesmerised hour watching the waves on a stormy day to see that it is

the sea that is breaking up the islands. The boom and shudder of waves

in sea-cut caves under your feet tells you about the corrosive power of wind

and water, as does the precarious cliff-edge perch of the Black Fort,

Dún Dúchathair.

LEFT Dignity in decay: a ruined gatehouse near Parkbane, Co. Clare.

LEFT A doorway at Dún Aengus, the
great clifftop fortress on Inishmore, in
the Aran Islands.

RIGHT Walkers brave the very lip
of these knife-edge cliffs, looking
west out to the sea.

anticipating when they sited the Black Fort to command the western approaches to the Aran Islands, an invincible stronghold on the brink of cliffs that themselves look impregnable?

The same questions came to mind an hour later as I picked my way through storm-flung stones along the cliff edge towards the dark silhouette of Dún Aengus. Like Dún Dúchathair, this great fortress stands on Inishmore's clifftops looking west, three concentric semi-circles of painstakingly cut and fitted stone blocks with doorways sharply defined. The ends of the curved walls of Dún Aengus are sliced off short at the very rim of the cliffs. It is as if Angus's Fort literally reflects the passing of time, its vanished half forming three ghostly semi-circles in mirror image out above the sea where long-tumbled cliffs once jutted. Or were the circles never unbroken, but deliberately designed as crescents butting snugly up to the wind on a 300ft void?

You have to pick your path with care as you approach the fort, for the builders laid a cunning minefield to trap the unwary. They sowed a shin-high chevaux de frise or thicket of sharp stone blades, wedged upright in cracks in the rock pavement, so that any attackers would be forced to advance at a slow walk and keep their attention on where they were placing their feet. Defenders on the walls of Dún Aengus, 20ft above, could select their targets at leisure and pick them off one by one as they stumbled through the obstacle.

From the walls of Dún Aengus I gazed south across Galway Bay to the long coastal profile of County Clare, where the Burren hills rose in pale grey domes. In the west the sea horizon lay flat. If the magical island of Hy Brasil was truly out there, as myth-makers down the ages have said, it was veiled beyond sight today.

FOLLOWING PAGE Sunlit beauty of
Roundstone Bay, one of the rare
sheltered harbours along the wild
Connemara coast.

I inched around the corner of the wall and got safely inside the fort. A wall is all that remains; a wall built 20ft high of stone blocks, furnished with stairs, walkways and lookout posts, enclosing the tip of the ever-diminishing promontory as a flat grassy bay. Here snakes a little labyrinth of low stone walls, a puzzle and a mystery to archaeologists who have tried to put a date to Dún Dúchathair. Was it built 2,000 years ago, or far further back in time? What kind of attack could the builders have been

YOU HAVE TO PICK YOUR PATH WITH CARE
AS YOU APPROACH THE FORT, FOR THE BUILDERS LAID
A CUNNING MINEFIELD TO TRAP THE UNWARY.

ABOVE Storm clouds lower over the Kerry hills, a spartan home to the early Christian hermits.

RIGHT Home for a pair of hermits? Ruined clochans way out west in Co. Kerry.

TOP RIGHT A latterday clochan on the Dingle peninsula, a careful reconstruction.

HERMITS OF THE CLOCHANS

The early Christian hermits clung like limpets to the storm-swept hill slopes at the western end of the Dingle Peninsula. They must have been tough, these adoptive Kerrymen, fortified by faith, subsisting on a diet of mountain plants and shellfish when things got really tough. And what you see of their dwellings, here at the heart of Ireland's greatest density of archaeological remains, reinforces the impression of lives of cheerless harshness. Between Ventry and Dunquin there must be several dozen hemispherical clochans, beehive-shaped stone huts with walls three feet thick and waist-high doorways sited away from the south-west wind. They look as comfortless as can be. Stooping to hobble inside one, and crouching there in the damp and dark, it is not hard to imagine what it must have been like on a wild freezing winter night in a gale of sleet.

Nearby in the hillside are the souterrains or underground storehouses that the Kerry saints excavated and lined with stone. Nowadays, as with the clochans, they contain fishing nets, cow dung or skulking sheep. The wind has blown earth

and sand to cover the open tops of some of the clochans, and seeded them with tufts of pink thrift or clover nodding in the eternal sea wind. From a little way off they look like giants with stony heads and jaunty flowered hats, buried up to their necks in the hillside.

HISTORY IN THE STONES

An ancient tower, rising out of the bleak limestone landscape of north-western County Clare. A blackened stone stairway rises to pass upwards and out of sight in a corkscrew of uneven stone steps. There are gaps in the spiral. One unwary footfall can easily lead to a broken ankle. You tread cautiously up through the five levels of Newtown Castle, poking your head through archways into intermediate rooms. The centuries-old ceilings are still imprinted with the criss-cross impressions of the wicker frames used by medieval plasterers to hold their handiwork up until it dried. The windows are blurred in outline, eaten ragged by the centuries of weathering. It is a long time since the O'Loghlens, 'Kings of the Burren', held sway here: longer still since the sixteenth-century O'Brien chiefs raised this gaunt tower.

The top of the stair comes out in a round room at the top of the castle, beautifully carpeted by nature with buttercups and forget-me-nots. You look out of the windows, sagging squares barred with half-rotted mullions, north over Ballyvaughan and Galway Bay, south across the bosomy grey limestone hills into the wild heart of the Burren.

In the pub last night the fiddle-player was telling you that Newtown Castle was about to be restored as a tourist attraction. He tried to give you directions south from the castle to find the forgotten ring fort of Cahermacnaghten, too, but sense of direction and sense of the ridiculous must have become confused somewhere among the pints. Eventually you find the fort, a crumbling ring of stone thirty paces wide, and you stand in the rain imagining the great days of the early sixteenth century when students and wise men flocked to Cahermacnaghten to teach and learn the ancient Celtic conventions, known as 'Brehon Law', on which Irish society was founded.

Cahermacnaghten had been a centre of learning since early medieval times, and the law school founded here around 1500 by the O'Davorens became the most influential of its kind. It had not been established half a century when King Henry VIII of England proclaimed himself King of Ireland. That act initiated the years of

ABOVE 'Their cattle are very fat, for the grass between the rocks is very nourishing.' General Ludlow, 1651.

RIGHT Monks' refuge from the Vikings: Kilmacduagh round tower, Co. Galway.

oppression that would culminate with Oliver Cromwell's ruthless crushing of the native west in the 1650s. General Ludlow, in his 1651 report to Cromwell, noted of the Burren that 'it has not any tree to hang a man, nor enough water to drown him, nor enough earth to bury him.' But, said the General, 'their cattle are very fat, for the grass growing in tufts of earth of two or three foot square that lie between the rocks which are of limestone is very nourishing.' Cattle still thrive on the Burren grass, and have carpeted Cahermacnaghten with enough dung to grow a dense crop of stinging nettles. No-one has lived there since the oppression. The rooms within the walls where Donald O'Davoren transcribed the prophecies of Conn of the Hundred Battles are tumbled to heaps of stones, and the whole structure looks set to go the same way before long.

You trudge on south and east from Cahermacnaghten. Perhaps your sojourn there has made you wiser, but at any rate you ignore

what the fiddler told you about this great short cut he knew over the hills to Leamaneh, and stick to the roads which get you there in a couple of hours as the rain sweeps off into Connemara and the tarmac begins to glisten stickily. At Leamaneh the castle ruins loom blank-eyed above a junction of roads. You can make out the original fifteenth-century O'Brien stronghold tower at one corner of the great four-storey mansion that was tacked on in the 1640s, at a time when precious few fine houses were being built in the Burren. Maybe there was special pleading in the case of Leamaneh, for its formidable chatelaine Máire Rua McMahon, Red-haired Mary, took an officer in the occupying army as one of her two husbands. She seems to have retained Leamaneh more or less intact. Nowadays it stands bleak and empty, its little round-arched doorway forming a moue of protest under ranks of sky-filled windows and a broken roofline, time and rural poverty having accomplished what Cromwell's men could not.

PRINT OF THE FAMINE

The Scardaun Valley at the heart of the Nephin Beg mountains lies five miles from any tarmac road or inhabited house. The Bangor Trail, that peat-sodden 'old and only pass into Erris', ribbons wetly along the Scardaun mountain slopes. The valley floor is a flat-surfaced bog, glinting with pools and lakelets. Ruins of houses flank the track on the hillside above, and the view down from these shattered former dwellings is of stripes and circles etched in the face of the bog. It takes a while to make out what they represent. The corduroy stripes were once lazybeds for growing potatoes, and the circles were cattle pens. The bog has the appearance of a photographic negative, retaining impressions

BELOW Leamaneh Castle in the Burren, ruined by time and rural poverty.

RIGHT The gentle landscapes of the south-east: Mayo's Nephin Beg Mountains reflected in Lough Feeagh.

of a time long gone. There are straight trackways printed in its surface, too, 'toghers' by which the inhabitants of Scardaun got around their lonely valley in the days before it emptied for ever.

The Reverend Caesar Otway travelled here on horseback in the 1830s, finding the Nephin Beg droving route horribly boggy. 'No mortal made carriage could ever have exercised wheel upon its track,' he wrote in his account, *Sketches in Erris and Tyrawley*. 'Who would venture on its unpleasant ways but the smuggler or the outlaw?' Even then the old toghers across the valley floor had been all but swallowed up in the bog. The Scardaun people had to drag their horses across on the end of a rope, while the well-bred mounts of Mr Otway and his companions snorted and jibed when faced with the crossing.

Life was rough and ready in the one-roomed cabins of Scardaun. The doorways were filled up with turf or creels to stop the wind blowing through. The entire family stripped off at night-time and lay down on the rush-carpeted earth floor under coarse

blankets, in a carefully regulated arrangement which ensured that the male visitors slept next to the sons of the house and as far away as possible from the eldest nubile daughter. Animals wandered in and out. But there was plenty of poteen to drink and eggs to eat, along with that reliable staff and staple of rural Ireland, the potato.

Neither guests nor hosts realised it, of course, but this bucolic way of life had only ten years left to run. In the autumn of 1845 the people of Scardaun, like several million other subsistence-level Irish peasants, opened their lazybeds to harvest the potatoes, and discovered only a mass of black slime inside. *Phytophthora infestans*, the potato blight fungus, had descended to wipe out the whole of the potato crop on which the entire population of rural Ireland relied for food.

The Great Famine would rage for five years, changing the life and politics and the landscape of Ireland for ever. A third of the population disappeared during the Famine. One million of these

ABOVE Old-style Connemara cottage, built of timber and stones from the bog.

RIGHT The Great Famine of 1845–9 left ruined villages and empty land all over Ireland.

BELOW Ruined cottage beneath a glowering sky on the Ring of Kerry.

died of disease and starvation. An ebb tide of emigration began, and continued to carry away the best and brightest youngsters for the next 150 years. The island's population shrank from nine million to three million, draining off the vitality of Ireland and emptying great tracts of the west. Bitterness against the clumsy and inadequate response of the British government to the disaster would spark upheavals and armed risings throughout the rest of the nineteenth century, and lead to the 1916 Easter Rising and to the War of Independence and the tragic Civil War that followed. Further down this line of cause and effect would be full political autonomy for the Republic of Ireland, and towards the end of the twentieth century the misery and heartless bloodshed of the Troubles in the north.

Scardaun emptied, and never refilled. Like dozens of other such places in rural Ireland, the poignant story of the Great Famine is still to be read here, written plainly in the print of abandoned lazybeds, tumbled cattle pens, sunken toghers and ruined houses that are only slowly fading from the landscape.

ROAD TO NOWHERE

We are driving between Lisheeneagh and Cooleabeg when Maryangela Keane suddenly says, 'Stop here a minute.' I pull the car over by a gatepost and we get out. 'See there?' says Maryangela. The top of the stone post is inscribed with a date: 1848. 'Fourth year of the Famine,' Maryangela murmurs, as if to herself. 'See the track there, leading off to nowhere? A famine relief work. I'll show you something, now.' We get back in the car and drive on a little way. 'Stop just here,' instructs Maryangela, and we climb out on to a windy hillside.

This track is a faint one, running off along the contour of the slope. It could be a well-trodden cattle path, except for a straightness to its course that can only be the result of human decision-making. Grass and orchids have taken hold along its surface, but beneath the beauty of their invasion the bare gravelly trackbed holds its integrity.

We set out along this famine road. It heads for the hills, going nowhere, its only justification the employment that its building gave to the starving peasants of the Burren during the Great Famine. Did they have to work for their handouts of food because

LEFT The outlines of the ridges where potatoes were grown are plain to be seen at Claggan, Co. Mayo.

ABOVE Once the deadly potato fungus had taken hold, the backbreaking labour of the 'lazybed' ridges was all in vain.

Victorian morality said you can't have something for nothing, I ask my companion, or because working removed the stigma of 'charity' from the relief? Maryangela shakes her head and doesn't give an opinion.

Every few yards a little mound of limestone chippings has been heaped neatly on the verge of the track. 'The women and children would break up the rocks as the men quarried them,' says Maryangela at my side, 'and reduce them to gravel for the road surface. Whatever wasn't used has just stayed here.' She taps one of the mounds gently with her toe. 'Little monuments, you know – monuments to all that suffering ...'

ON THE RELIEF WORKS, 1905

'At a turning of the road we came in sight of a dozen or more men and women working hurriedly and doggedly improving a further portion of this road, with a ganger swaggering among them and directing their work. Some of the people were cutting out sods

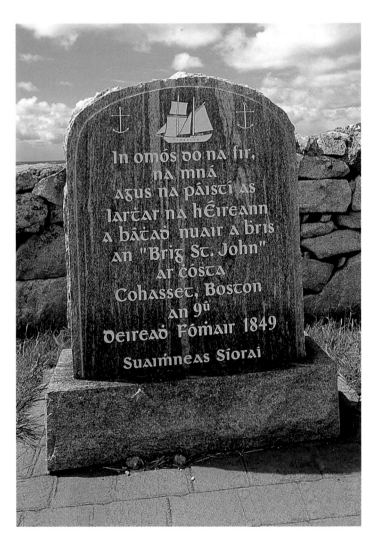

from grassy patches near the road, others were carrying down bags of earth in a slow, inert procession, a few were breaking stones, and three or four women were scraping out a sort of sandpit at a little distance. As we drove quickly by, we could see that every man and woman was working with a sort of hang-dog dejection that would be enough to make any casual passer mistake them for a band of convicts. The wages given on these works are usually a shilling a day, and as a rule one person only, generally the head of the family, is taken from each house. Sometimes the best worker in a family is thus forced away from his ordinary work of farming or fishing or kelp-making for this wretched remuneration at a time when his private industry is most needed. If this system of relief has some things in its favour, it is far from satisfactory in other ways, and is not always economical. I have been told of a district not very far from here where there is a ganger, an overseer, an inspector, a paymaster, and an engineer superintending the work of two paupers only. This is possibly an exaggerated account of what is really taking place, yet it probably shows, not too inexactly, a state of things that is not too rare in Ireland.'

TOP LEFT Commemorating the innocent victims of the famine: Gorumna Island sculpture.

BOTTOM LEFT Another poignant memorial on Gorumna Island in Galway Bay.

ABOVE The characteristic landscape of the Burren: domed hills of naked limestone, rising from pastoral valleys.

LEFT Fishing nets and dry stone walls, symbol of the Aran Islands of Connemara.

RIGHT Looking from Dunquin across the turbulent waters of Blasket Sound toward Great Blasket Island.

The playwright John Millington Synge, commissioned by the Manchester Guardian in 1905 to report on conditions in the Congested Districts of Connemara, pulled no punches in his dispatches to the newspaper. Neither did his fellow-reporter Jack Yeats, artist-brother to poet W.B. Yeats, whose pen and ink drawings show hollow faces, eyes burning with fever, ragged clothes and figures slumped in despair. Yet the scenes that Synge and Yeats recorded in southern Connemara were taking place a good half-century after the Great Famine had officially ended in 1849.

The trouble was over-population, that curse of remote districts of Catholic Europe. Too many mouths to feed, too little workable land to support them. Nowhere was the situation more dire than in the granite-pocked boggy islands of Lettermore, Gorumna and Lettermullan and their satellite islands that hang in a ragged chain from the north coast of Galway Bay. Today you can drive through the archipelago along a ribboning road that leapfrogs the narrow sea gaps between the islands on stone-built causeways. The islanders built them in bitter labour to earn their shillings in the desperate years around 1900.

Most haunting of all Jack Yeats's illustrations was the drawing that appeared in the Manchester Guardian of 21 June 1905. It showed the toothless ferryman of Dinish Island, wizened and wasted but rowing his boat with sinewy strength, the black holes of his eye sockets lit by two sickly sparks. The modern observer of the drawing has difficulty in believing that this ancient, fevered scarecrow is only 57 years old. His wife is dead, he has young children and nothing to feed them on, his cows and pigs have been sold, and he is desperate for the move to America that he cannot make because he has no money and because his children are too young for him to think of leaving them.

'If it wasn't for them,' he tells Synge as he rows the strangers over to Dinish, 'I'd be off this evening. But how can I leave my young children? I don't know what way I'm to go on living in this place that the Lord created last, I'm thinking, in the end of time, and it's often when I sit down and look around on it I do begin cursing and damning and asking myself how poor people can go on executing their religion at all.'

TEACH SYNGE

I knock on the door of the tidy little house on Inishmaan, remotest of the Aran islands. Dia dhuit, God be with you, I say to the bespectacled lady who answers the door. Do you think I could look round Teach Synge? Well, she says, Teach Synge is private. But you can look round.

LEFT Old traditions of home life and
work persist for the cottagers on the
Aran Islands.

RIGHT Tradition in architecture;
slate may have replaced thatch,
but the single-storey, three-room
cottage endures.

Teach Synge, the 'House of Synge', stands behind her cottage. It
is a long, low house, rather neglected, its whitewash grubby, its
thatch green with grass tufts and moss clumps. I go in at the
green-painted door, and find myself in what was once the
kitchen. In spite of the heaps of stored fishing net that half-fill
the little room, and the mouldy condition of the yellow and blue
walls, I recognise the place. At this blackened fireplace John
Millington Synge would sit hour after hour, listening to the tall
tales of the rheumatic old story-teller Pat Dirane or watching the
movements of the island women and men as they went about
their eternal tasks of making and mending. The House of Synge
was the home of the McDonagh family when the playwright
came to lodge here each year between 1898 and 1902. He was
gathering material for newspaper articles that he would soon
publish in the form of the classic account, *The Aran Islanders*,
and sifting the idiosyncratic Inishmaan islanders' Gaelic dialect
and mindset for nuggets of inspiration for the plays he was
brewing, *The Playboy of the Western World* and *Riders to the Sea*.
Back then the islanders still lived lives all but indistinguishable
from those of their forefathers, and as a consequence were in
great demand as teachers and exemplars by the scholarly and
romantic nationalists of the turn-of-the-century Gaelic revival
movement. Synge was rather more matter-of-fact, though
equally passionate, in the delight he took in everyday life at
McDonagh's:

'The kitchen itself, where I will spend most of my time, is full
of beauty and distinction. The red dresses of the women who
cluster round the fire on their stools give a glow of almost Eastern
richness, and the walls have been toned by the turf smoke to a
soft brown that blends with the grey earth-colour of the floor.
Many sorts of fishing tackle, and the nets and oil-skins of the men,
are hung upon the walls or among the open rafters; and right
overhead, under the thatch, there is a whole cowskin from which
they make pampooties (skin shoes).'

I push folds of fishing net aside and peep through the kitchen
door into an austere little bedroom with green-painted walls. Here
Synge could withdraw from the kitchen fireside to enjoy some
privacy while still feeling himself part of the household, as on a
miserable fog-bound evening when a little sovereign remedy
seemed called for:

'This evening the bottle of poteen was drawn from its hiding-
place ... their grey poteen, which brings a shock of joy to the
blood, seems predestined to keep sanity in men who live,
forgotten, in these worlds of mist. I sat in the kitchen part of the
evening to feel the gaiety that was rising, and when I came into
my own room after dark, one of the sons came in every time the
bottle made its round, to pour me out my share.'

I daydream through Teach Synge, picturing the playwright and
the poteen, as full of romantic fantasies as any floppy-haired
Gaelic revivalist. The key-holder recalls me to reality by letting
slip that she herself is the granddaughter of J.M. Synge's landlady,
Mrs McDonagh, and that if anyone might be looking for a plot of
land to build a new house on ... well, Teach Synge is really past
repair anyway, isn't it? Yes ...

LEFT Padraic Pearse's cottage: the foundations of independence for Ireland were laid here at Rosmuc in the Connemara bogland.

BELOW RIGHT A rainstorm charging inland across Lough Oiriulach, near Padraic Pearse's house, leaves a spectacular rainbow in its wake.

PADRAIC PEARSE AND THE ROSMUC COTTAGE

The Connemara road dips to the granite-encrusted shores of Lough Oiriúlach, under a curious little hillock. The thatched cottage on this knoll, immaculately painted and freshly and impeccably thatched, looks unassuming, even when I climb up to it. I pay a minimal entrance fee and walk through the plain bedrooms of the little house with their purgatorial wooden bedsteads. Everything here is neat, stripped and orderly. It would please Padraic Pearse, could he see the house he built in the Rosmuc bogland still so plain and unadorned, its message of self-discipline and austere living so unsullied.

There is an irony here, for this seemingly untouched interior is a careful reconstruction. The original was torched in 1921 by Black and Tans, members of the paramilitary regiment let loose in Ireland by the British Army at the time of the War of Independence. Pearse had been dead for five years by then, executed by firing squad in Kilmainham Jail for his part in the Easter Rising of 1916. The Dublin schoolmaster-poet died in unofficial office as President of the self-proclaimed Irish Republican Government. It was he who read out the proclamation of the new republic from the steps of the GPO in O'Connell Street on that fateful Easter Monday:

'... We hereby proclaim the Irish Republic as a Sovereign Independent State, and we pledge our lives and the lives of our comrades-in-arms to the cause of its freedom, of its welfare and of its exaltation among the nations.'

Fine phrases, which led Pearse and his fellow rebels to the execution yard within ten days. They also led, five years and thousands of deaths later, to the proper establishment of that independent state. The ideas behind them were honed in this

'WE HEREBY PROCLAIM THE IRISH REPUBLIC AS A SOVEREIGN INDEPENDENT STATE, AND WE PLEDGE OUR LIVES AND THE LIVES OF OUR COMRADES-IN-ARMS TO THE CAUSE OF ITS FREEDOM.'

little cottage on the knoll above Lough Oiriúlach, where I now lounge and flick through a book of short stories by Pearse. Set in this harsh landscape of southern Connemara, high-mindedly moral and imbued with Christian principles, they scarcely seem a manifesto for bloody revolution. Pearse was a dreamer of dreams, who would invite his Dublin pupils to the cottage in order to soak their young minds in Irish mythology, poetry, customs and language. He became a man of action, a member of the Supreme Council of the Irish Republican Brotherhood by 1915, an advocate of armed uprising and the central figure of the whole republican movement. But the humble Rosmuc cottage and the traditional life of the countryside around it were the bedrock of his inspiration, the foundation to which he would

return time and again in order to get his feet back on the ground of ordinary Irish life.

I pay for the paperback of Pearse's stories and slip it into my rucksack, then descend from the knoll to the shore road again. A group of youths scuffles towards me, boisterously. 'Dia dhuit, God be with you,' I greet them, anticipating blank stares, perhaps open hostility to the stranger and his clumsy attempt at communication. 'Dia agus Mhuire dhuit, God and Mary be with you,' they murmur. We pause to chat. They are Dubliners, over in Connemara brushing up their Gaelic at summer school. Padraic Pearse? Yes, aye, he was kind of a great man. But do I have a fag on me? Jesus, it'll be great to get back to Dublin out of all this feckin' bog, so it will ...

Chapter 7

OLD AS THE HILLS

'FAITH YOU SEE –
THE OLD FAITH...'

Believer in Cures and Holy Wells, Kilmoon, Co. Clare

The Janus Man stands among daffodils in the old cemetery on Boa Island.

The calm water of Lower Lough Erne glints through the trees, and there is a

quiet backwash of birdsong. There are no signs or explanations for the Janus

Man; you have to take him as you find him, which is in a state of phallic

upswing. He is a squat little man of stone with wide-bulging eyes, as if daring

you to stare too closely.

Round the other side of the stone you find his twin brother, also carved

with leaf-shaped staring eyes and half-open mouth. This Janus Man has a pair

of braces crossed on his chest – or perhaps they are two stick-thin arms – and a

belt around his waist. He is neatly bearded, a pointed imperial like that of an

Elizabethan explorer. But the Janus Man would have been at least a thousand

years old when Sir Francis Drake was circumnavigating the world.

LEFT Enigmatic stone circles at
Beaghmore: the Tyrone bogland
conceals many more such
archaeological treasures.

In the top of the stone between the two brothers is a mossy hollow, filled with rainwater. Sacred vessel for pagan anointings; receptacle for sacrificial blood? I dip the tip of my finger into the little rain pool, and watch the sky tremble and subside.

SILENT SEVEN

Two or three miles east along Lough Erne; two or three centuries of time passed since the Janus Man was made. The seven stone figures on White Island must have been carved in very early Christian times by someone with biblical knowledge, though what exactly he was getting at is as hard to fathom as the riddle of the Janus Man. In modern times the figures have been disciplined, built into a stone wall in a well-drilled rank that somehow enhances their individual eccentricity.

The left flank of the file is guarded by a grinning, monkey-faced sheela-na-gig holding apart the lips of her vulva. Her neighbour is a seated man, also smiling, with something that could be a book laid on his knees – possibly a figure of Christ preaching out of the Gospels. The five figures that follow are twice the size of this left-side pair. First comes a priest or saint with a cowl over his head, holding a bishop's crook in his right hand and a bell in his left; then a figure that some think is the Boy David with a shepherd's rod, his left hand pointing to his mouth as if to signify the beautiful singing voice that so enraptured King Saul. Next in line is a curly-haired hero with weirdly staring eyes, perhaps a representation of Christ vanquishing evil; he grips a pair of gryphons by the neck so that their eagle beaks are jammed together tip to tip. Then comes a soldierly Christ figure with a short sword and round target shield. Last in line is a stone dressed for sculpting, the shape of head and body roughed out but not worked into any detail. The right side of the rank is closed by a small scowling head, probably carved several centuries after the Seven.

They stare out boldly, challenging all comers to read their coded messages: the point at which Christian and pagan melt together.

THE MONASTERY THAT BUILT ITSELF

Down along the lakeside road, ten miles south, you reach another of Lower Lough Erne's holy islets. The great round tower of Devenish Island beckons like a slender grey finger, but the boatman takes his own good time to ferry you over from Trory

jetty. Devenish is a place where time hangs suspended. Didn't Saint Molaise himself, 'little flame the beautiful from multitudinous Devenish', sit for a hundred years listening to the birds sing while the monastery magically built itself around him? So the legends say, though the monks who laboured so hard to erect the churches, the towering belfry under its cone cap and the finely carved High Cross on the summit of the islet might have had another story to tell.

Molaise died in 563 AD, and the island monastery he founded in Lough Erne wielded its influence for the next thousand years until the Cromwellian suppressions. The island became the peace-making and negotiating capital of medieval Ireland; the historic

ABOVE The overgrown ruins of Castle Caldwell on Lough Erne, Co. Fermanagh.

RIGHT The Janus Man of Boa Island in Lough Erne: there are no signs or explanations of its meaning.

peace accord of 1259 between Ulster and neighbouring rival Connacht was one of those forged here at the monastery on 'Devenish of the Assemblies'. Not that everyone who came to Devenish came in peace. Viking marauders sacked the place in 837. In 1157 'Devenish with its churches was burned,' according to contemporary accounts – possibly by accident, but probably by Norsemen, since the monks immediately set about building their great round tower.

You climb up rickety ladders, as the monks themselves must have done, through the trapdoors of four successive floors, to emerge in a little cylindrical room under the stone cap. From the slit windows you look out across the shells and restored shapes of the monastery's churches, away beyond Devenish over the island-

spattered waters of Loch Erne. Or you can dream back down the parallel perspectives of the ladders to a crack of sunlight in the half-open door of the tower nearly a hundred feet below, and picture the monks of the Irish monasteries during the grim centuries of Dark Ages raids as they sealed themselves into their towers and waited prayerfully and fearfully to hear axe-blows thundering on the door and the first crackle of flames.

MUIREDACH'S CROSS

Beautifully preserved on the stone shaft of the thousand-year-old Muíredach's Cross, at Monasterboice in County Louth, are carved biblical scenes. Adam and Eve stand in a conspiratorial huddle under the fruit-laden boughs of the Tree of Knowledge. Next to them are their sons, fixed mid-quarrel, with a stiff-backed Cain beating his brother Abel on the head with a cudgel. Shepherd boy David confronts a fat-faced Goliath. A crowd of Israelites in two well-ordered ranks watches Moses smite a fountain from the desert rock. The Wise Men (there seem to be four of them) crouch uncomfortably, packed down like a rugby scrum, as they adore the infant Jesus in Mary's arms. Above them, at the hub of the cross wheel, Christ the Supreme Judge adjudicates on Doomsday. On his right the Saved stream towards him, all holding hands, while on his left the Damned turn away in despair as they are pitchforked off to Hell. Beneath his feet the Archangel Michael weighs a soul in a balance: it passes the test, even though the Devil, crushed as he is at the Archangel's feet, is trying to tug down the scale to his advantage. Above all these lively scenes of murder, mayhem and salvation, two saints – perhaps Paul and Anthony – share communion in a little one-roomed chapel under a neatly tiled and steeply gabled roof with an elaborately grooved ridge.

MILK FOR THE MASONS

Up in County Tyrone, on the western shore of Lough Neagh, more intricate carvings survive on the 18ft High Cross at Ardboe. This tenth-century cross, more exposed to the elements in its lakeside setting than Muíredach's Cross in the shelter of the Monasterboice

YOU CLIMB UP RICKETY LADDERS,
    AS THE MONKS THEMSELVES
MUST HAVE DONE, TO EMERGE
    IN A LITTLE CYLINDRICAL ROOM
        UNDER THE STONE CAP.

ABOVE The ruined buildings of the
Dark Ages and medieval Christian
settlements dot the islets in Lough
Erne, Co. Fermanagh.

buildings, is also more weathered. But it is not difficult to make out Cain belting Abel on the head with a flail, Daniel with two splendid lions parading on their hind legs, King Solomon delivering his judgement on the disputed baby (which is being held upside down like the Pig Baby in *Alice in Wonderland*), and the money changers in the temple grouped round a table unaware that Christ is about to kick it over.

Any local worth his salt can tell you why Ardboe High Cross has been strong enough to stand for well over a thousand years. The masons who erected it worked up a thirst that could not be slaked by any secular beverage. So St Colman of Dromore, whose earthly remains lie in the monastic cemetery at Ardboe, caused a cow to walk across Lough Neagh to bring milk to the workers. The miraculous cow gave so much milk that the masons could not drink it all, so they mixed what was left over with the mortar they were preparing. This divine addition made the mortar strong enough to hold up the High Cross until Judgement Day.

People hereabouts have a reverence for the great High Cross. A funeral tradition says that the coffin had to be carried round the cross three times before it could be buried. Pre-Christian practices still attach to this spot, too. Near the cross stands a Wishing Tree, stone dead, poisoned by the thousands of copper coins pushed deep into its trunk and limbs by those who prefer older and more arcane forms of worship and petition.

PRIEST'S LEP

The lane rose by twists and curls to a high pass, where it tipped from Kerry over into Cork. 'Priest's Leap', the pass was labelled on my map.

'I'll tell you,' said the woman who came to her farm gate to greet the stranger and call off her dogs. 'That story has been passed down through the generations, you see, until it came to me.

'It was in the days of the penal laws, you know, when Catholics in this country were not let to say Mass. The soldiers were hunting priests like dogs; they caught one in the valley below there, and didn't they kill him when they caught him? Anyway, the people had what we call a Mass rock up there, a kind of an open-air chapel on the hill. This other priest was above at the rock there, saying Mass, and didn't the soldiers come for to catch him. So he ran out ahead of them, and away with him to the top of the road with the Host in his pocket and the soldiers behind. There was a horse that the people had waiting up there.

BELOW A modest metal cross marks the spot at Priest's Lep from which the persecuted Mass celebrant made his famous horseback jump all the way to Bantry.

RIGHT The bare stone-walled landscape of Inishmore, where priest and school teacher fought for supremacy at the turn of the 20th century.

"Get up, Father," they said, "up now!" So this priest jumped up on the horse and he lepped out off the rock, and didn't the horse land in Bantry ten miles away! And so the place has had the name of the 'Priest's Lep' ever since.

'Now when that horse landed in Bantry he left the marks of his hooves in the rock. You can see them there today, just on the side

beside the road. They were tarring that road a little while back, and they covered up the hoof marks with the tar. But when they came back the next morning the tar had turned aside, and weren't the marks there as clear as ever!'

THE PRIEST AND THE PEDAGOGUE

Parish priest and schoolteacher: in pre-independence Ireland, and especially in remote outposts, these two literate men with their trained minds could rule the roost in a largely illiterate rural society. What they decided, by and large, was what happened, for better or worse. If priest and teacher got along and could work together, they might have a profound influence for good in their community. It could be a very different story if two such powerful figures came into conflict.

In his 1932 novel *Skerrett*, Liam O'Flaherty drew a thinly fictionalised picture of what happened when the schoolteacher and the priest clashed at the turn of the twentieth century on the author's native Inishmore, largest of the three Aran Islands. O'Flaherty had been a pupil of the teacher in question, David O'Callaghan, and had attended the church of Father Murty Farragher, parish priest of the islands, so he was in a good position to witness the conflict as it unfolded. David O'Callaghan ('David Skerrett', as O'Flaherty calls him) was a hot-tempered and spiky man, a romantic nationalist and fervent advocate of the virtues of the Gaelic language and traditional island customs. Father Farragher ('Father Moclair'), on the other hand, is shown as a progressive, an ambitious pragmatist who understood that modernisation of the islands would advance his career and feather his nest.

The two men were absolutely as chalk and cheese, temperamentally and ideologically. Their bitter disagreements divided the islanders and soured the atmosphere. There had to be a winner, and it was the accomplished tactician Father Farragher. O'Callaghan, his position made untenable, lost everything. The priest had him sacked. The schoolteacher's house went with the job, and so David O'Callaghan was forced to leave the island in ignominy after serving the community there for 34 years.

INSURANCE POLICY

A howling grey morning on Inishmaan, with the island under attack. The wind tears at the fleeces of the sheep, bowls the lobster creels about, trembles the stacked currachs by the pier, and sends house-high waves furrowing over the sound from Inisheer to explode on Inishmaan's eastern shore with a deep bass thump that one feels rather than hears.

Things are snug enough in the church, though, where we are at morning Mass. I share my bench with an island man who wears jacket and trousers of homespun cloth. His dog is curled up sound

LEFT A worshipper with his rosary at the ready at Knock shrine, Co. Mayo.

asleep on the floor between us. There are a few younger women in the congregation, dressed fashionably or casually according to inclination, but most of the twenty or so people present are elderly island women with square-patterned headscarves drawn tightly over their hair. The full skirts of their homespun and home-sewn dresses of red and blue wool swish softly as they rise, sit and kneel, and their rosary beads click gently as a counterpoint to their murmuring. It is a soporific atmosphere, what with the soft murmuring and clicking and the low dreamy moan of the wind outside. I am struggling to keep awake, partly because the crack in Inishmaan's pub was mighty last night (and early this morning), and partly because the Mass is being conducted in Irish of which I only understand four or five phrases.

It is Father Raymond's last Mass on Inishmaan. The genial and full-bearded stand-in priest is due to leave the island today, his locum stint finished. Inishmaan will miss his fiddle playing and enthusiastic singing, and especially his tall tale-telling – also his gentle voice and manner.

Father Raymond may speak softly, but he carries a big laugh. We hear it full strength in the cramped nine-seater Islander plane later in the day. Father Raymond and a substantial lady sit jammed together haunch to haunch. If they should each take a deep breath at the same moment, they will burst the plane apart. The island woman grips Father Raymond's arm with her right hand and crosses herself with her left as the little plane shudders at the end of the grass airstrip. The priest fumbles in his jacket

LEFT Ancient art, unchanging vision: Celtic cross at Clonmacnoise monastic site, Co. Offaly.

pocket and pulls out a small glass bottle. A nice drop of the 'cratur', to steady the nerves? Not exactly. From his other pocket Father Raymond extracts a little instrument like a painting brush with floppy bristles, and dips it into the bottle. Then he flicks it vigorously back and forth, showering everyone – pilot included – with holy water. 'Insurance policy!' chuckles Father Raymond, and roars with laughter as we bounce and lurch up into the purple storm clouds over Galway Bay.

THE THIRD REALITY

'What people maybe don't realise,' says Father Michael Liston, parish priest of Cratloe village, 'is that in Ireland there is what I call the third reality. There's the first reality, which you might

ABOVE A sample of the humours of Knock: painted bottles of holy water are offered for sale.

LEFT A signpost in Knock: holy water and confessions for the crowds of visiting faithful.

call organised religion, the whole structure of church and Mass, the hierarchy of priests and bishops, rules and laws of the Roman Catholic church that everybody takes in with their mother's milk. There's the second reality of life as it is actually lived day-to-day, modern secular life. And then in Ireland there is this third reality, which is a really deep and strong feeling for the Christian religion that somehow operates together with and yet apart from the other two realities. It works away below the surface, underneath, all unseen – a great tide of faith in action, flowing at a very deep instinctive level.'

ABOVE An innocent devotion: children at their First Communion at Killorglin, Co. Kerry.

TOP RIGHT A roadside shrine at Corrofin in the Burren, Co. Clare – a common sight in rural Ireland.

VISION AT CARNS

If you were looking for the absolutely typical small Irish village, the kind of rural community where the most exciting event is a tractor that won't start, Carns on the Mayo/Sligo border would do very nicely. Carns is probably the last place on earth, or at least in north-west Ireland, that anyone would expect the Mother of God to reveal herself to four teenage girls. Yet that is what happened on a September evening in 1985. According to their account, the girls were walking home together from the shop. It was a dark night, so the apparition of Our Lady shone out clearly as she stood twelve feet tall in a roadside field, cowled in a white veil, with a bright star shining beside her head. St Bernadette was with her, said the girls, and the two figures followed the awed quartet until they reached home.

The girls told their secret to a trusted few the following day, and thirty gathered in the field next night to witness the miracle. The Blessed Virgin did not seem put out by the crowds that swelled night after night: she continued to reveal herself, culminating in a spectacular event on the seventh night. Three thousand had assembled, and their experiences were many and varied. Some saw the figure of Our Lady and smelt the sweet scent of roses, some beheld a cross, or a vision of the Sacred Heart of Jesus shedding drops of blood. To some it was as if the sky split open to reveal a dazzlingly bright light; others had the impression of an orange star shooting clear across the sky.

Mass hysteria? Wishful thinking? Cunningly staged pyrotechnics? Could the independent witness of three thousand onlookers really be dismissed as a phenomenon of group psychology? And did what was happening in Carns really matter anyway? The church authorities floundered around, unwilling to credit the events, unable to reject them outright. Meanwhile the country people of Mayo and Sligo continued to visit the field. Some experienced further visions, others saw nothing. No conclusions could be drawn.

As for the four girls: the visions quickly stopped, and they resumed the obscurity – and the security – of teenage in Carns.

PRAYERS IN A BASEBALL JACKET

Midday at St Bridget's Well near Lough Gill in County Sligo. A big statue of Jesus on the cross stands high on a bank among trees. A blue-shawled Virgin Mary keeps her Son company. There are votive candles alight in the stands beyond the well's pool of dimpling water, endlessly alive with gentle currents. A young man

BELOW Both the Christian and the older
faith are nourished by the rhythms of hard
work and celebration in agricultural Ireland.

of twenty dips a jug in the water, drinks a mouthful, and blesses himself with the sign of the cross made with a wetted fingertip. Then he bows his head to pray – not a wild-eyed fanatic figure by any means, but an ordinary youth in jeans and a baseball jacket who has ridden his bike out from Sligo town during his lunchbreak because the action of paying this short visit to the holy well comes as naturally to him as breathing.

PREVIOUS PAGE Croagh Patrick, the Holy Mountain, climbed by Ireland's believers each Garland Sunday.

BELOW Standing stone as a scratching post: archaeological monuments are everyday objects in the fields of Co. Mayo.

THE WELL ON THE SHORE

A thyme-scented boreen on Gorumna Island, a grass-grown lane thick with purple bell heather and blue buttons of scabious, leading me down to lonely Lough Tan. The shore of the lake is deserted, but when I get to the triangular cleft in the granite rock that local people call Tobairín Naomh Anna, St Anne's Little Well, I can see that I am not the first here this morning. Bunches of fresh flowers have been propped in crevices of the stone wall that guards the spring. Also here, pushed into interstices, are cheap holy pictures, rosaries and religious statuettes. Pill bottles and pairs of spectacles lie as offerings, discarded as the holy well's

cures have taken effect. 'Will you say a prayer for me there?' a woman asked me an hour ago as she gave me directions to find St Anne's well, and I am only too happy to oblige as the lough water laps quietly and the whistle of an osytercatcher comes up from a sea inlet nearby.

THE OLD FAITH

A path beside a stone field wall near Kilmoon in County Clare: not a public right of way, but well enough used to be marked out strongly in the grass of the pasture. At first sighting the stone structure on the back slope of the hill looks like a farmer's toolshed, but as I come closer I can see a short flight of steps descending into darkness inside. Brown water stirs at the bottom of the steps, welling up among ferns. A niche holds tiny, crudely coloured pictures of the Virgin Mary and of Christ. Old iron horseshoes, home-made crucifixes and strips of rag have been

ABOVE A well-tended shrine dedicated to St Bridget, one of Ireland's best-loved saints.

pushed into gaps between the stones of the wall that enfolds the holy well of St Colman. Fresh flowers picked no earlier than this morning have been brought to beautify this secret little resource out in the fields.

A few yards off, the circular summit of a shallow hillock is a sea of mud. In the centre rises a square-framed arch of stone perhaps eighteen inches wide, its cracked upper edge a foot above the ground. It looks like the frame of a small window, the sort of thing you might expect to find in the wall of some ancient oratory or monastic cell. Now that I look more closely, I can see that the mud around the arch is indented with dozens of saucer-shaped impressions, as if a succession of people has knelt there.

LEFT Faiths ancient and modern: pre-Christian standing stones in the Mayo bogland, with the cone of St Patrick's holy mountain rising beyond.

RIGHT A sign of the continuity of faith; a Celtic cross at Burrishoole Abbey, Co. Mayo.

'And did you put your head through the arch yourself?' enquires the old man whom I find waiting for me when I get back to the road again. 'You didn't? Well, that's how you'd cure your headache. There would be dozens round here use the old well and the arch. Faith, you see – the old faith. There's a young crowd that's coming up now doesn't believe in anything like that. 'Tis the television, do you see – television has them ruined altogether.'

STONES OF LANKHILL

Certain places resonate: there is no better word for it. Take the field of Lankhill, on the ancient pilgrimage route from Ballintubber Abbey to the holy mountain of Croagh Patrick. Just beside the stile lies a miniature stone circle, some Bronze Age burial site. Over to the left rises a magnificent standing stone, its surface incised with whorly spirals, its profile cracked into the zigzag shape of a lightning flash that jags dramatically into the ground. Behind the stone, the crumbled walls of an early monastic cell are enfolded in a blackthorn's grasp.

The centre of the field is taken up by a thicket of trees. Inside stands the circular rampart of an Iron Age fortification, its interior seeded with dozens of mossy stones set upright in the earth: the uninscribed nameless gravestones of victims of the Great Famine, perhaps, or the clandestine burial place of illegitimate infants, consigned to the protection of the fairy circle in the extremity of desperation according to country custom. To one side rises a rough cube of stones, a mossy table under the trees. On the underside of a peculiarly flat stone that lies loose on top of this altar-shaped mound a crude cross is incised. The stone mound is an altar indeed; it was one of the secret Mass rocks where Catholics would gather in concealment during the eighteenth century, when the harsh Penal Laws

CONCEALED IN THE MIDDLE OF THE MOUND IS A BLADE OF STONE INCISED WITH SPIRALS – THE MISSING SEGMENT OF THE PAGAN STANDING STONE.

forbade them the right to attend a formal church celebration of
their religion's central mystery.

But this Mass rock is not founded on Christian faith alone.
Concealed in the middle of the mound is a blade of stone incised
with spirals – the missing segment of the pagan standing stone,
slyly smuggled into the very heart of this Christian altar.
Two trees twine their limbs below the Mass rock in the form of a
crucifix, and at their feet green stones shape the retaining wall of
a sacred well. A niche pierces the wall, and way back in the manmade cleft is the smoothness of a quartzite pebble. Sometimes the
cure-stone of Lankhill is there; sometimes it is not. If the niche is

PREVIOUS PAGE The 5,000-year-
old burial mound at Newgrange,
where winter solstice brings
momentary sunlight to the
hidden chamber.

LEFT A young girl fills her bottle
with holy water from a fountain at
Knock shrine, Co. Mayo.

BELOW LEFT One of the natural
monuments of Ireland that many find
as awe-inspiring as the manmade.

RIGHT The windswept cemetery at
Ventry on the Dingle peninsula,
Co. Kerry.

FOLLOWING PAGE Ventry Bay:
not the worst place in the world
to be buried.

empty the round white pebble is out at work, packaged up by some local person within the circle of such knowledge and posted off to Sydney, Australia, or Moose Jaw, Canada, or wherever in the world a fellow Mayoman or Mayowoman is suffering an affliction of the head. Somewhere an expatriate, or the descendant of a County Mayo emigrant, will ease physical pain or mental torment with the stone. Soon it will be posted or carried back to Mayo to be restored to its lichened bed in the old well wall, plugged back into a source of healing too recondite to respond to scientific enquiry. It works, or it doesn't. You believe, or you don't. Faith, you see – the old faith …

LEFT Olcan Masterson draws inspiration from Mayo's rocks and seas.

RIGHT The Giant's Causeway on the Antrim coast – built, some say, as stepping stones by the hero Fionn MacCumhaill so he could visit his giantess girlfriend on Staffa Island.

FOLLOWING PAGE The sun goes down over a serene Clew Bay, with Achill Island sinking into the mist.

'WE BURY THEM WELL HEREABOUTS'

The graveyard stood among dunes, between the long white curve of the strand and the breaking wave of Mount Eagle. A strong Atlantic wind rushed through the grasses and whipped at the headscarves and suit jackets of the mourners. The priest's words were snatched from his lips and scattered to the north like sand.

It was a man from Caherantrant they were burying this morning, 88 years old, never been out of the Dingle peninsula, so the woman beside me whispered. 'Not the worst place in the world to be buried,' I said, watching green rollers pushing in across Ventry Bay and hearing the pipe of curlews from the mountain. 'Yes,' she murmured, looking round, 'we bury them well hereabouts.'

RIDING THE BEAM

It is just before nine o'clock on a cold December morning, the shortest day of the year. The great round burial mound stands silently on its frosted white hill, its portal open to the east. At the heart of the tomb, in the three clover-leaf chambers and the domed hall at the end of the sixty-foot stone-lined passage, the silence is profound. Each chamber contains a wide stone dish, empty. They have held no ashes of cremation for thousands of years.

A finger of the rising sun has been stretching steadily towards Newgrange and now touches the portal. It penetrates the slit above the entrance and moves along the stone gullet of the roof box. The orange finger reaches the ice-cold core of the mound, probing forward until it comes to rest in a smeary glow of light on the back wall of the furthermost chamber. There it hovers for a few frozen minutes, every moment of its residence freighted with magic.

The glow slides down the chamber wall, glides back across the hall floor, fading as it withdraws. A collective breath outpours from the watchers who have been crouching spellbound under the dome. There is a sense of diminution, a reluctance to let the light go. If they could grasp the tip of the glowing finger of light and halt the withdrawal, they would.

Yearning and delight adhere to the light as it retires, leaving the heart of Newgrange to another year's darkness as it has done for 5,000 years. Perhaps the builders of Newgrange knew that it was the souls of their dead, year by year, who rode the beam out of the mound and over the horizon to roll back the darkness and bring on the spring.

DANCING WITH OLCAN

Olcan and I pass into the clouds. Loose rubble clinks beneath our boots as we labour up the cone-shaped mountain. Our lungs burn, we spatter the stones with sweat. Mist pearls in our hair and runs down our faces.

We laugh weakly with exhaustion and glee as we stumble to the chapel on the summit of Croagh Patrick. Olcan shakes my hand vigorously, then flings his arms round me in a bear hug. Now is the moment when the clouds should part, and miraculously they do. The Connemara mountains roll away southward. North across the island-dotted waters of Clew Bay rise the peaks of Nephin Beg. Out in the west, a watery sun lies on the green hump of Clare Island.

Olcan and I dance around, a waltz of elation. Then he takes off his knapsack, draws out his black whistle and, still breathless, he begins to play 'Old As The Hills'.

THIS BOOK IS DEDICATED WITH LOVE
TO MY WIFE JANE

ACKNOWLEDGEMENTS

Grateful thanks, as always, to my good and hospitable
friends in Ireland, including Margaret Gallagher of Mullylusty,
Gussie Russell and Teresa McGann of Doolin, Didi Korner and
Anne Kelly of Island More in Clew Bay, Derry and Conal and
other fine ramblers of Dublin, Lord John McGing of Westport,
Oliver Geraghty of Newport, Tom Joyce of the Slieve Blooms, Jack
Buckley of Cork, Maryangela Keane of the Burren in Co. Clare,
Michael Gibbons of Clifden, Tim Robinson and Malachy Bodhran
of Roundstone, Pat Dooley of the Offaly boglands, Pat O'Hagan of
Cookstown, Owen Smith and Declan Forde of Fernagh in Tyrone,
Nuala Enright of Sixmilebridge, Johnny McKeagney of Tempo,
Jim Hoy of Derrygonnelly, and Olcan and Shari Masterson of
Belclare in Mayo; also Katrina Doherty of Bord Failte and Orla
Farren of the Northern Ireland Tourist Board for all their
cheerful efficiency. Christopher Somerville

The blue skies, the rain, the green hills, the crashing seas, the
music and most of all, the warmth of the welcome were an
inspiration for my photographs. A thank you to everyone who
helped me to capture some of Ireland's spirit. Chris Coe

The poem 'Ferrying her over' (quoted on p.43) is extracted
from Christopher Somerville's first collection of poems,
Extraordinary Flight (The Rockingham Press, 2000 –
ISBN 1-873468-69-5)